ENTEBBE
The Most Daring Raid of Israel's Special Forces

SIMON DUNSTAN

New York

This edition published in 2011 by:

The Rosen Publishing Group, Inc.
29 East 21st Street
New York, NY 10010

Library of Congress Cataloging-in-Publication Data

Dunstan, Simon.

Entebbe: the most daring raid of Israel's special forces/Simon Dunstan.

p. cm. — (The most daring raids in history)

Includes bibliographical references and index.

ISBN 978-1-4488-1868-6 (library binding)

1. Entebbe Airport Raid, 1976—Juvenile literature. I. Title.

DS119.7.D8629 2011

967.6104'2—dc22

2010029622

Manufactured in the United States of America

CPSIA Compliance Information: Batch #W11YA: For further information, contact Rosen Publishing, New York, New York, at 1-800-237-9932.

CONTENTS

INTRODUCTION

The Origins of Aerial Hijacking

The first airline was founded on November 16, 1909, in Frankfurt, but it was only in the wake of World War I (1914–1918) that commercial air travel began in earnest. The maiden flight of what was considered to be a truly modern airliner took place in February 1933: a twin-engine Boeing 247 monoplane that was capable of flying from coast to coast across the United States of America in just 20 hours. The following month, on March 28, 1933, the first airline disaster caused by an act of sabotage occurred when an Imperial Airways Armstrong Whitworth Argosy crashed in flames in the Belgian countryside near Dixmunde, some 60 miles (97 kilometers) northwest of Brussels. All 15 passengers and the crew of three were killed. It was not the only incident that year. On October 10, 1933, a United Airlines Boeing 247 flying from Cleveland, Ohio, to Chicago, Illinois, was destroyed in midair by a nitroglycerine explosive device, killing all seven persons on board.

In the late 1940s, a number of civilian airliners were hijacked as people in Eastern Europe attempted to flee communist rule. However, the first act of political terrorism against a commercial airliner occurred on April 11, 1955. An Air India International Lockheed 749A Constellation carrying Chinese delegates and journalists was disabled by an explosive device and crashed into the South China Sea with the loss of 19 lives.

The first of a series of aerial hijackings involving Cuban aircraft took place on April 9, 1958. Such incidents increased significantly following the Cuban Revolution and the assumption of power by Fidel Castro in 1959, with the standard destination being Miami, Florida, with its large Cuban population. In the early 1960s, no U.S. federal law against aerial piracy had yet been implemented. As a result, a number of lone gunmen hijacked American domestic flights, instructing the pilots to change course for Cuba, the landing place of choice for hijackers of aircraft originating in South America, Central America, and the Caribbean at this time.

Although there had been remarkably few casualties or fatalities among crews or passengers of hijacked aircraft, the first losses in the USA since the advent of the jet age were reported on board an Eastern Airlines DC-9 Series 31 airliner, designated Flight 1320, on March 17, 1970. A single gunman burst onto the flight deck, shooting the two pilots. Despite being mortally wounded, First Officer James Hartley overpowered and shot the hijacker with his own pistol and, notwithstanding his severe injuries, Capt Robert Wilbur was able to land the aircraft safely.

Prior to the Six Day War of June 1967, aerial hijackings and sabotage were comparatively rare in the Middle East. However, the humiliating defeat suffered by the Arab world during this conflict galvanized the various Palestinian factions into independent action. On July 23, 1968, members of the Popular Front for the Liberation of Palestine (PFLP) hijacked an El Al Boeing 707-458 bound for Tel Aviv from Rome. Flight 426, having initially set out from London, was carrying 38 passengers and a crew of ten when Capt Oded Abarbanell radioed that he was being forced to fly to Algiers. After landing at Dar el Baida Airport, the passengers were divided into Jews and gentiles, the latter being immediately released. After five days of frustrating negotiation, ten Israeli women and children, including three air stewardesses, were released. The other hostages were freed some five weeks later, after the Israeli government agreed to an exchange of 16 political prisoners. El Al, Israel's national airline, subsequently introduced the most rigorous security measures possible to protect its aircraft and passengers. Armed security guards known as "air marshals" were now routinely carried on flights, while all luggage was hand searched and the aircraft flight decks protected by armored doors. Israel also instituted a policy of retaliation for any attack against its citizens in the biblical tradition of "an eye for an eye."

These measures were even more meticulously implemented following an attack on an El Al Boeing 707-358B at Athens Airport in Greece on December 26, 1968. As it taxied down the runway for takeoff, two PFLP terrorists riddled the airplane with automatic fire. One passenger was killed and a stewardess wounded, while the aircraft was badly damaged. Both terrorists were captured and imprisoned. Two days later the Israeli Defense Forces (IDF) mounted Operation *Tshura* (Reward) in response, targeting aircraft of Middle Eastern countries located at Beirut International Airport. Under the command of BrigGen Rafael "Raful" Eitan, three assault units were

In September 1970, the PFLP hijacked four airliners in a dramatic act of air piracy. The aircraft were flown to a remote desert airstrip in Jordan at al-Azraq but known as Dawson's Field, since it was formerly a RAF wartime base. To the PFLP hijackers, it became "Revolution Airport." On September 12, the PFLP destroyed the empty aircraft with explosives in an orgy of destruction leading to armed confrontation between the PLO and the Hashemite Kingdom of Jordan. (Photo by Getty Images)

gathered at Ramat David, an air base near Nazareth, on December 28, 1968. Each unit, comprising approximately 22 men, was assigned a sector of the airport and tasked with destroying as many aircraft as possible that could be readily identified as belonging to Arab airlines or the Lebanese Air Force. The assault force was inserted by six Israeli Air Force Aerospatiale SA 321K Super Frelon *Tzir'a* helicopters of No. 114 Squadron (*Tzir'a* being Hebrew for "Hornet"). Seven Bell 204 helicopters supported the operation and, in case it became necessary to evacuate by sea, four Saar class missile boats and naval commandos of Shayetet 13 also made up the detachment. The first helicopter landed at 2118hrs, and, within 30 minutes, 14 aircraft had been destroyed: 13 belonging to Middle East Airlines and one, hit by mistake, to Ghanaian Airlines. The wreckage included two Boeing 707-320Cs, three de Havilland Comet C4s, one Sud Aviation Caravelle, and one Vickers VC10, with the remainder being Vickers Viscount turboprop airliners. The estimated damage caused was in the region of $45 million. The policy of "an eye for an eye" was now firmly established.

The PFLP launched a further automatic weapons attack against an El Al Boeing 720B as it was about to take off at Zurich-Kloten Airport in Switzerland on February 18, 1969. The aircraft was hit some 40 times, and a trainee pilot was killed. The PFLP struck again on August 29, 1969, with the hijacking of Trans World Airlines Flight 840 en route from Rome to Tel Aviv. The Boeing 707-331B was diverted to Damascus Airport in Syria, where the aircraft was destroyed by an explosive charge. All on board were released except for six Israelis who, some three months later, were exchanged for 13 Syrian military prisoners held by Israel.

And so the cycle of terrorism and aerial hijacking continued, but by now the security measures instituted by El Al made their aircraft far more difficult to seize. Furthermore, the Israeli government had introduced a policy of no longer exchanging political prisoners for hostages, irrespective of whether they were of Jewish origin. Consequently the terrorists sought easier targets such as airlines belonging to the Western powers that supported Israel. They also adopted other means of circumventing Israeli security measures, using a network of international terrorist groups to penetrate Israeli defenses more successfully.

Black September

On September 6, 1970, the PFLP orchestrated the simultaneous multiple hijacking of airliners of various nationalities in order to gain maximum worldwide publicity for the Palestinian cause. The airplanes, all of which were bound for New York, included a Pan American World Airways (Pan Am) Boeing 747-121, a Trans World Airlines Boeing 707-331B, and a Swissair McDonnell Douglas DC-8 Series 53. An attempted seizure of an El Al Boeing 707 failed when the pilot, Capt Uri Bar-Lev, flung the aircraft into a steep dive, throwing both hijackers off balance; they were then overpowered by the flight attendants and an air marshal, and one of the assailants, Patrick Arguello, was shot dead. Three days later a British Overseas Airways Corporation (BOAC) BAC Super VC-10 was hijacked soon after takeoff from Bahrain while en route from Bombay (modern day Mumbai) to London.

The Pan Am Boeing 747 was flown to Cairo in Egypt, where it was blown up in front of the world's media as a protest against the Egyptian government's participation in peace talks with Israel (held in an attempt to end the war of attrition along the Suez Canal). The other three aircraft were flown to a former Royal Air Force (RAF) World War II airstrip named Dawson's Field in Jordan. After summoning the world's press, the three airliners were destroyed in a series of spectacular explosions. All the passengers were released unharmed. However, this brazen violation of Jordanian sovereignty was too much for the Hashemite Kingdom, and King Hussein ordered the expulsion of the Palestine Liberation Organization (PLO) and its Arab acolytes. In a bitter civil war lasting until July 1971, almost 8,000 people were killed, with thousands of Palestinians being forced to flee to Lebanon, where the PLO set up new bases. Yasser Arafat's prestige as chairman of the PLO was severely harmed by the events of September 1970. In response, he set up the Black September terrorist group to perpetrate further outrages; ensuring it was totally separate from the PLO, he could then deny links with any future attacks. Its name was taken from the dark days of defeat in September 1970, and the first victim of this new organization was the Jordanian Prime Minister Wasfi Tel. He was assassinated on the streets of Cairo on November 28, 1971, in retaliation for the expulsion of the PLO from Jordan.

The Black September group bided its time. Then, on May 8, 1972, a Sabena Boeing 707-329 with 101 passengers flying from Brussels to Tel Aviv was hijacked by two men and two women shortly after takeoff from Vienna. After landing at Lod (later known as Ben Gurion) Airport in Tel Aviv, the hijackers demanded the release of 317 *fedayeen* (freedom fighters) held in Israeli jails. The Israeli government demurred but offered the release of fewer prisoners while it considered a military response. Meanwhile, mechanics based at the airport had deflated the tires of the aircraft in order to prevent its departure. With the arrival of Minister of Defense Moshe Dayan and IDF Chief of Staff David Elazar, the IDF's elite Special Forces unit, Sayeret Matkal, was ordered to formulate a plan to storm the aircraft. The following day, the hijackers demanded that the aircraft be made serviceable by mechanics under the supervision of officials of the International Red Cross Committee (IRCC). Carrying bulky toolboxes, the ground crew in their white overalls approached the Boeing 707 and were searched by the Red Cross team. The "mechanics" then retrieved the tools of their trade from their hiding places and burst onto the aircraft with pistols and Uzi submachine guns. The two male hijackers were dispatched with gunshots to the head, and one of the females was wounded. Despite orders to stay down, one Israeli woman passenger jumped up in panic and was shot in the head; she fell mortally wounded. The assault had lasted just 90 seconds.

Bereaved parents and relatives mourn at the graves of their teenage children murdered by DFLP gunmen at Netiv Meir School in Ma'alot on May 15, 1974, Israel's Independence Day. On the following day, as the funerals were taking place, 36 aircraft of the Israeli Air Force swept in from the Mediterranean Sea and dropped 250 tons (227 metric tons) of ordnance on various camps and targets across Lebanon, killing 27 and wounding 138. In Beirut, the fallen fedayeen were honored as noble martyrs of the cause in demonstrations orchestrated by Nayef Hawatmeh, the DFLP leader.

PALESTINIAN PARAMILITARY GROUPS

FATAH

It remains a truism that one man's terrorist is another man's freedom fighter. The latter is called "fedayeen" in Arabic, which also translates as "self-sacrificing."

For the Palestinians, the Second Arab-Israeli War of 1956 reaffirmed the failure of conventional Arab armies to confront Israel. Herded into overcrowded and unsanitary camps and towns since 1948, they felt betrayed by the world. All the Arab states except Jordan denied the Palestinians either citizenship or equal rights in their respective countries. Determined to advance their own cause, the Movement for the National Liberation of Palestine was formed by Yasser Arafat and a group of fellow Palestinian exiles in Kuwait. Taking the name al-Fatah, or "conquest by jihad," in 1959, the group was backed by Syria as another tool in the confrontation with Israel. Fatah began fedayeen/terrorist operations inside Israel from January 2, 1965. Arafat was highly critical of the Pan-Arab nationalism espoused by Colonel Gamal Abdel Nasser of Egypt. Accordingly the latter orchestrated the formation of the Palestine Liberation Organization, or PLO, during the Arab Summit of January 1963 with the intention of usurping the influence of Fatah but with the pretense of presenting a unified political entity for all Palestinian refugees.

Typical of Palestinian politics, the PLO soon split into various mutually distrustful factions of differing ideologies and methodologies in their ambition for the liberation of Palestine. Notable among these groups were the Popular Front for the Liberation of Palestine (PFLP), the Democratic Front for the Liberation of Palestine (DFLP), and the Popular Front for the Liberation of Palestine—General Command (PFLP–GC)—all of a Marxist-Leninist persuasion. The internecine rifts continued for years resulting in only limited confrontation with the main enemy of Israel. In 1965, the PLO launched just 35 terrorist raids against Israel; in 1966 some 41, and in the first four months of 1967, 37 attacks were undertaken. In 1967, Yasser Arafat maneuvered Fatah into the ranks of the PLO and became its chairman two years later, a position he held until his death in 2004. During that time, Arafat steered the PLO from being mainly a liberation/ terrorist movement to become the quasi-legitimate political body representing the aspirations of the Palestinian cause in the eyes of the world. Yet this policy has led to the loss of much of the PLO's credibility within the Palestinian people and allowed the rise of more committed/extremist groups such as Hamas in the Gaza Strip, although Fatah still holds sway in the West Bank.

PFLP

The Popular Front for the Liberation of Palestine was a secular, Marxist-Leninist paramilitary group that was formed in 1967 after the Six Day War. Sponsored by Syria, it was the second largest in size after Fatah with some 3,000 fedayeen in 1968. Dr. George Habash, a Palestinian Christian, led the group but, unlike Yasser Arafat, he remained wedded to the concept of Pan-Arabism as the means to counter Western imperialism and the state of Israel. The PFLP were the leading proponents of aerial hijacking during the late 1960s and into the 1970s, including the multiple hijacking of four airliners to Dawson's Field in Jordan on September 6, 1970.

PFLP–GC

The Popular Front for the Liberation of Palestine—General Command was formed in December 1968 following an ideological split with George Habash of the PFLP. Backed and controlled by Syria, the PFLP–GC was led by a former Syrian army officer, Capt Ahmed Jibril, who was a fierce opponent of Yasser Arafat although the group remained within the PLO until 1974. As a soldier, Jibril soon tired of the endless Marxist-Leninist rhetoric and philosophizing and advocated direct military action against Israel, hence the impressive title of PFLP–General Command with the promise to the Palestinians of "a gun in every hand." In February 1970, the PFLP–GC was responsible for the destruction of a Swissair flight from Zurich to Tel Aviv, and in April 1974 perpetrated the first suicide bombings at Kiryat Shimona in northern Israel when three guerrillas killed themselves and 18 hostages with explosives.

DFLP

On February 22, 1969, the Democratic Front for the Liberation of Palestine broke away from the PFLP to pursue a Maoist political doctrine. Led by the extreme left-wing Naif Hawatmeh, the DFLP was based in Syria and supported armed insurrection against Israel. Fortunately, the group engaged in interminable heated discussions on such vexed questions as to whether there should be a hyphen in "Marxist-Leninism" that it did not undertake terrorist attacks against Israel until 1972. Nevertheless, the DFLP committed

one of the most awful atrocities within Israel when on May 15, 1974, three fedayeen launched a devastating attack against a school in Ma'alot that resulted in the deaths of 25 people, mainly students, during an unsuccessful hostage rescue mission by IDF Special Forces.

PRFLP

In February 1972, the Popular Revolutionary Front for the Liberation of Palestine emerged following a further split in the PFLP over the events of Black September. This splinter group was led by Abu Shibab, a former Politburo member of the PFLP. The PRFLP was supported by Fatah in Yasser Arafat's continuing ideological struggle with George Habash of the PFLP. Arafat also had problems with his deputy, Wadia Haddad, to such an extent that he was expelled from the PFLP whereupon he formed the Popular Front for the Liberation of Palestine—External Operations or PFLP–EO.

PFLP–EO

Within the PFLP, Dr. Wadia Haddad had been the commander of its military wing and was instrumental in forming the strategy of aerial hijacking in order to head-line the Palestinian cause on the world stage. He was the mastermind behind the multiple hijackings to Dawson's Field in September 1970 that led to the expulsion of the PLO from Jordan. Accordingly, he was ordered by the PLO and the PFLP to stop aerial hijackings, but he continued to do so under the aegis of the Popular Front for the Liberation of Palestine—External Operations. In order to distance the Palestinian leadership from international terrorism, Haddad increasingly sought the assistance of external terrorist groups such as the West German Red Army Faction or Ilich Ramirez Sanchez, better known as Carlos the Jackal, with whom he organized the assault on the OPEC conference in Vienna on December 22, 1975. As part of the PFLP–EO, there were several subgroups such as the PFLP–SO, or Special Operations, and PFLP–SOG, or Special Operations Group. It was under the banner of the PFLP–SOG that the West German terrorists of the *Revolutionäre Zellen,* or Revolutionary Cells, were recruited to undertake the hijacking of Air France Flight 139 while Wadia Haddad controlled the overall operation from Mogadishu in Somalia.

THE HIJACKING OF AIR FRANCE FLIGHT 139

The primary aim of terrorists is to instill fear and uncertainty in the society they wish to destroy. Attacks are often indiscriminate with civilians a key target, such as this school bus that was destroyed on March 18, 1968. As the bus was leaving the Wadi Raham following a visit to the Red Canyon tourist site in the Eilat Nature Reserve, it struck a mine laid shortly before by fedayeen infiltrators. Two men were killed outright—a teacher, Dr. Pesach Maylen, and a guard, Hanan Kalev—and 28 pupils of the Herzeliya School were wounded, some of them severely. It was just one attack among many, but the result was always lives extinguished or traumatized forever.

Operation *Uganda*

Following the expulsion of the PLO from Jordan and the disastrous failed seizure of the Sabena flight, the leader of the PFLP, George Habash, renounced the hijacking of aircraft as counterproductive; he felt it did more damage to the Palestinian cause internationally than any advantage gained from publicity. Others disagreed, causing a split in the movement, with the PFLP deputy, Wadia Haddad, forming the Popular Front for the Liberation of Palestine—Special Operations Group (PFLP–SOG) that was still committed to the hijacking and destruction of Israeli and Western airliners. After the outbreak of the Lebanese civil war in 1975, many PLO leaders deemed it sensible to leave Beirut and find safer locations farther afield. Wadia Haddad and the PFLP–SOG relocated to the People's Republic of South Yemen, where PLO training areas had been established in a location deemed to be beyond the range of Israeli retribution. The main bases were at Hanf, Al-Gheida, and Mukalia. They were staffed and supplied by approximately 1,500 Soviets together with 700 Cuban and 116 East German advisors and instructors. Since security on El Al airliners was now so tight and was improving all the time at many Western airports, Haddad decided to attack an Israeli aircraft from an unexpected quarter.

In January 1976, three members of the PFLP–SOG called on the British consulate in Beirut to obtain visas to visit Kenya (whose diplomatic affairs in Lebanon were conducted by Britain). Unknown to the three Palestinians, they were under surveillance by Mossad, the Israeli Secret Service. Traveling on false passports, they arrived in the Kenyan capital of Nairobi where, on the 18th, they were arrested on the perimeter of Nairobi's Embakasi Airport following a tip-off from Mossad. In their possession were two Strela SAM-7 shoulder-fired surface-to-air missiles. Under interrogation by the Kenyan Security Service General Service Unit (GSU), they admitted to a plot to shoot

down an El Al airliner. They also revealed that agents of President Idi Amin of Uganda had supplied the SAM-7 missiles and the weapons found in their hire car. As the questioning continued in secret, Haddad dispatched a West German couple, Thomas Reuter and Brigitte Schulz, to discover the whereabouts of his operatives. When they were subsequently arrested on arrival in Nairobi, these two members of the Red Army faction were carrying further plans to attack El Al aircraft. Having thwarted the attacks, the GSU handed over the five terrorists to the Israelis and they were subsequently tried, convicted, and imprisoned for their crimes. However, the plot marked a new departure for international terrorism with aircraft now vulnerable to attack in any part of the world. It also saw close cooperation between Mossad and the Kenyan GSU that was to be of considerable importance in the near future. Despite the failure of the Nairobi attack, Wadia Haddad was confident that another operation already in an advanced stage of planning, codenamed *Uganda*, would grab headlines around the world.

Day 1: Sunday June 27, 1976—"We Have a Hijacking"

Just four months later, at 0645hrs on June 27, 1976, Singapore Airlines Flight 763 from Singapore landed at Athens Airport after a stopover in Bahrain, where two Arabs had boarded the aircraft under the names of Fahim al-Satti and Hosni Albou Waiki. They were in fact senior members of the PFLP–SOG whose real names were Fayez Abdul-Rahim Jaber, one of the founders of the PFLP, and Jayel Naji al-Arjam, Deputy Chief of the PFLP–SOG Foreign Relations Department. Also on the flight were two West Germans traveling on South American passports. Using the aliases of Señor Garcia and Señora Ortega, Wilfried Böse and his former girlfriend Brigitte Kuhlmann were members of the urban guerrilla group *Revolutionäre Zellen* (Revolutionary Cells). Böse was a close associate of Ilich Ramirez Sanchez, better known as Carlos the Jackal. Sanchez had fallen out with Wadia Haddad over the recent kidnapping of oil ministers from the Organization of the Petroleum Exporting Countries (OPEC), and so Carlos himself had no connection with Operation *Uganda*. Baggage handlers at Bahrain had ensured the weapons and hand grenades in their hand luggage were smuggled onto the aircraft undetected. In the broiling summer heat of the Athens Airport transit lounge, they waited patiently for their connecting flight. At 0859hrs, Air France Flight 139, an Airbus A300B4-2C (F-BVGG) with Capt Michel Bacos at the controls, took off from Lod Airport in Tel Aviv. Carrying 228 passengers, the plane was bound for Paris via Athens. At 1130hrs, Flight 139 touched down at Ellinikon Airport, where 38 passengers alighted and another 56 boarded the aircraft for Paris. The aircraft now carried 246 passengers and a crew of 12.

The PFLP–SOG had selected Athens Airport because of its notoriously poor security measures, and so it proved to be on Sunday June 27. The metal detector was unmanned, and the official working the hand luggage X-ray machine was paying little heed to his duties. All four terrorists boarded the Airbus without hindrance. At 1220hrs, Air France Flight 139 took off, but some minutes later, screams were heard in the first-class cabin. In a matter of moments, the aircraft had been seized with Brigitte Kuhlmann controlling events in first class and the two Palestinians taking charge in economy. A pilot of 21 years' experience, Michel Bacos later recounted: "Seven minutes after departing from Athens we heard screams on board. We thought there was a fire in the cabin. The flight engineer, Jacques Le Moine, opened the cockpit door and I found myself face to face with a man." Wilfried Böse had burst onto the flight deck wielding a pistol and a hand grenade. Bacos continued: "The terrorist had his gun pointed continuously at my head and occasionally he would poke my neck not to look at him. We could only obey the orders of the terrorists." It was the first hijacking in Air France history.

Kuhlmann made an announcement over the aircraft public address system declaring that the flight was now under the command of the *Che Guevara Group and Gaza Unit of the Popular Front for the Liberation of Palestine*, with a new call sign of "Haifa One." Having made himself familiar with the flight controls of the Airbus A300, Böse ordered the pilot to head for Libya while Kuhlmann verbally abused the passengers and pistol-whipped anyone who showed signs of resistance. One Frenchman was punched to the floor and severely beaten. Packages, supposedly of explosives, were placed in the aisles and around the emergency exits. Once subdued, each passenger was searched for weapons. Their passports and any identification papers were then confiscated and scrutinized. Sarah Davidson was traveling to the United States with her husband, Uzi, and their two sons, Ron and Benny. As a reserve navigator in the Israeli Air Force, Uzi slipped his military ID out of his shirt pocket, and both he and Sarah chewed it into a pulp, slipping the remains into an empty cola can just moments before a terrorist took their passports.

Within minutes of the hijack, Israeli electronic monitoring units became aware that all radio transmissions from Flight 139 had ceased. The information was immediately passed to the prime minister, Yitzhak Rabin, during a routine cabinet meeting. Deep underground in the Kirya headquarters of the IDF, the duty officer gave the Sayeret Matkal cell the news: "We have a hijacking—an Air France plane out of

THE SAVOY HOTEL ATTACK

The failure of the Special Forces to save the victims of Ma'alot came as a blow to the prestige of the IDF. It was battered further following a terrorist outrage in the heart of the nation's capital of Tel Aviv masterminded by Khalil Al-Wazir, better known as "Abu Jihad" meaning "Father of Jihad" and a founding member of Fatah. At 2330hrs on the night of May 4, 1975, eight al-Assifa raiders (meaning "Storm," the al-Assifa were the elite fighters of the military wing of Fatah) landed on the beaches of Tel Aviv from rubber dinghies: the methodology was particular since this operation was in revenge for

the death, in Operation *Springtime of Youth,* of Muhammad Youssef Al-Najjar, a close friend of Khalil Al-Wazir. Unable to locate their primary objectives of the Manshia youth club and the Tel Aviv opera house, the terrorists chose a target of opportunity at random—the Savoy Hotel on Guela Street. Three people were killed in the initial assault, and many others were taken hostage. They were all barricaded in the top floor of the hotel, along with a couple that hid in a cupboard throughout the ordeal. The terrorists demanded the release of 20 Palestinians held in Israeli jails and an aircraft to transport them and the hostages to Damascus; all within the next four hours or else the hostages would be killed. The Sayeret Matkal implemented an immediate action plan and stormed the building at 0420 hours. In the ensuing firefight, eight hostages were killed and 11 wounded

while five were released unharmed, including the couple in the cupboard. During the action, three IDF soldiers were killed, including a former Sayeret Matkal commander, Uzi Yairi, who had fought with distinction during the battle of Chinese Farm in the Yom Kippur War. Seven of the terrorists were killed and one captured; some of them dying when they retreated to a room and blew themselves up with explosives. The unhappy outcome of the Ma'alot and Savoy Hotel operations led to a stringent reappraisal of Sayeret Matkal doctrine and procedures in counterterrorism. New techniques were introduced with specialized teams being trained to storm schools, houses, apartment blocks, planes, trains, and buses—indeed any target that terrorists might capture. But no one could envisage a target over 2,000 miles (3,219 km) away.

Greece. It took off from Tel Aviv earlier this morning." At 1327hrs, Sayeret Matkal (also known as "The Unit") was put on alert with the expectation that the hijacked aircraft would return to Tel Aviv. At 1458hrs, Flight 139 landed at Benghazi Airport in Libya. The Airbus was parked on a remote runway while the local PFLP representative negotiated with the authorities. There it remained in the fearsome heat. As the sweltering conditions worsened, one passenger, Patricia Martel, pretended to be pregnant and feigned a miscarriage by cutting herself severely enough to convince a Libyan doctor that she should be allowed to leave the aircraft. Eventually the Libyan authorities provided 42 tons (38 metric tons) of fuel, and after nearly seven hours on the ground, Flight 139 took to the air again at 2150hrs on the evening of June 27.

Into Africa

Prime Minister Yitzhak Rabin, meanwhile, convened a crisis management team comprising himself and five members of his cabinet, including Minister of Defense Shimon Peres, Foreign Minister Yigal Allon, Justice Minister Haim Zadok, Transportation Minister Gad Yaakobi, and Minister without Portfolio Yisrael Galili, as well as the Chief of Staff of the IDF, LtGen Mordechai "Motta" Gur. The first meeting began at 1605hrs with the news that Flight 139 had landed at Benghazi, confirming everyone's fears that this was indeed a hijacking. Since the Airbus belonged to Air France, it was quickly decided that Yigal Allon should approach his opposite number at the Quai d'Orsay and persuade the French government to take the lead in any negotiations with the terrorists to obtain the release of the hostages. At the same time, Gad Yaakobi was to seek the assistance of the international civil aviation authorities, as well as liaise with the families of the hostages. Needless to say, all branches of Israeli security were put on high alert in case Flight 139 returned to Israel, including Sayeret Matkal that was standing by at Lod Airport. With the news that the Airbus had landed in Benghazi, The Unit stood down but continued to refine a potential attack plan. Meanwhile, in the event the plane would remain in Libya under the protection of Col Muammar Qaddafi, the Operations Branch of the IDF was also involved in contingency planning. A small team comprising Maj Amiram Levine of Sayeret Matkal, Maj Gadi Shefi, the commander of Shayetet 13, and Maj Ido Embar from the Israeli Air Force Branch for Combined Operations formulated several options, which included punitive action that could be taken against Libya for its support of terrorist groups.

When news came that Flight 139 was airborne once more, The Unit was again placed on high alert. The final attack plan to storm the airliner was presented to MajGen Yekutiel "Kuti" Adam, the Chief of Operations Branch and Deputy Chief of Staff of the IDF, and his assistant Col Avigdor "Yanush" Ben-Gal (formerly the commander of the 7th Armored Brigade that had defended the Golan Heights during the 1973 Yom Kippur War against overwhelming odds). The briefing was repeated for Defense Minister Shimon Peres and his entourage when they arrived at Lod Airport at 0130hrs on Monday June 28. But as the night wore on, it was evident the aircraft was flying southeastward into the heart of Africa. The Unit and the other security forces were ordered to return to their bases. Throughout the five-hour journey, the passengers had to endure a constant torrent of abuse from Brigitte Kuhlmann, much of it anti-Semitic in nature. As the Airbus continued its flight, the Israeli government was still unsure as to the motives or demands of the hijackers. A rumor of a telephone call from Damascus to the Reuters News Agency in Kuwait was circulated, claiming that the Special Operations Group of the PFLP had hijacked the aircraft. Then came definite information from London. During the

JUNE 27, 1976

1225hrs: Air France Flight 139 seized by hijackers.

JUNE 27, 1976

1327hrs: Sayeret Matkal placed on alert.

course of the evening, Libyan Airlines had flown Patricia Martel back to Britain. As soon as she had landed at Heathrow Airport, she was interviewed by Scotland Yard and a representative from the Israeli embassy. She was able to confirm that there were four hijackers and, from photographs of convicted terrorists and suspects, that two of them were Germans.

Idi Amin and His Support for the Palestinian Cause

At 0315hrs on Monday June 28, Flight 139 made its final approach into Entebbe International Airport. Once it had taxied to a halt, powerful searchlights were trained on the aircraft, and armed Ugandan soldiers surrounded it. Another agonizing delay of nine hours ensued until the Airbus was moved to the Old Terminal, where all the passengers and crew finally disembarked. There they were confined in the former departure lounge. Some years previously, Entebbe Airport had been modernized with a new terminal, control tower, and runway constructed some 1.5 miles (2.4 km) away. Consequently the Old Terminal was dusty, dirty, and dilapidated, as well as being plagued by persistent midges (a small species of fly). Ugandan soldiers now guarded the hostages as the hijackers relaxed and met up with accomplices already in the country. Among them were Fouad Awad, a known associate of Carlos the Jackal, and a further two members of the PFLP–SOG, Abdel al-Latif and Abu Ali. They came equipped with a cache of weapons, including Kalashnikov assault rifles and more hand grenades. A former Lebanese army officer, Fouad Awad, was in command of the PFLP–SOG forces at the airport while overall control of the operation remained in the hands of Wadia Haddad at a forward headquarters in Mogadishu. As Sarah Davidson observed: "The terrorists felt sure of themselves. We were trapped in their hands like a mouse in a cat's paws."

During the course of the afternoon, the president of Uganda, Idi Amin, arrived by helicopter. He greeted the hostages with jovial cries of "*Shalom! Shalom!*" but the mood soon changed when one of the hostages posed a question and addressed him as "Mr. President." Several eyewitnesses later recalled that he flew into a rage at this point and insisted on being addressed as "His Excellency Field Marshal Doctor Idi Amin Dada." Resplendent in camouflage battle fatigues and accompanied by his

During the 1960s, Israel had close commercial relations with several African nations, particularly in the field of agriculture. Here, the prime minister of Israel, Levi Eshkol, pays an official visit to Uganda on June 12, 1966. In the background is the terminal building where the hostages were held some ten years later with the control tower to the left. To the left of the dais is the chief of staff of the Ugandan armed forces, Maj Gen Idi Amin, while to the right is the Ugandan vice president, John Babiha. Intriguingly, the dais is positioned in the same spot as the Air France Airbus was parked outside the Old Terminal during the hijacking.

similarly attired eight-year-old son, Idi Amin berated the hostages and insisted that only Israel could resolve the crisis by acceding to the hijackers' demands. Any hopes the hostages may have held that the president of Uganda would intercede on their behalf were quickly dashed. Throughout the day, attempts by the French Ambassador to Uganda, Pierre Renard, to negotiate with the hijackers came to naught. Ironically, Israel and Uganda had enjoyed cordial relations for several years prior to Idi Amin's seizure of power. During the 1960s, the Israelis had provided agricultural expertise, assisting in the cultivation of new cash crops to feed the burgeoning population, as well as for export. After Ugandan independence from Britain in 1962, the IDF had sent a military mission to train Amin's most loyal army battalions as paratroopers and to instruct the nascent Ugandan Air Force. Indeed, the self-styled field marshal wore Israeli paratrooper wings on his chest even though he had never made a single jump. Accused of misappropriating Ministry of Defense funds as chief of staff of the Ugandan armed forces, Gen Idi Amin immediately staged a coup against President Milton Obote on January 25, 1971, and declared himself head of state.

Initially Israel supported the president and increased its military presence in Uganda with the provision of Fouga Magister jet aircraft and surplus Sherman tanks. Idi Amin was even given the honorific Hebrew title of *Hagai Ne'eman* ("Reliable Helmsman"). Major civilian projects included a plan to develop water resources in the arid northern region of Karamoja by the Israeli company Tahal, and the improvement of Entebbe Airport with the construction of a modern terminal by another Israeli company, Solel Boneh. But within months, all political activity was banned in Uganda, and Amin instituted a ruthless military dictatorship whose abuses of civil and human rights became increasingly embarrassing to the Israeli government. Relations cooled between the two nations when Israel refused to provide monetary loans or assist Idi Amin militarily in his ongoing border disputes with neighboring Kenya and Tanzania. Unsurprisingly, his request for F-4 Phantom fighter bombers and other sophisticated hardware was turned down. Uganda now owed tens of millions of U.S. dollars for military equipment and

Once Israel and Uganda established diplomatic relations in 1962, Israel provided much needed expertise in many fields. In August 1963, four Ugandans qualified as pilots in Israel. By 1965, Israel was providing extensive training and equipment, including Piper Super Cub and Piaggio aircraft for the nascent Ugandan Air Force. Following attacks from Congolese aircraft against western Ugandan villages in 1965, Uganda received six armed Fouga Magister jet trainers and three DC-3 Dakota transport aircraft from the IAF. Israel also established training schools for Ugandan pilots, artillery officers, and paratroopers. By early 1967, Israel had seconded approximately 50 instructors to support this training mission, including officers such as Maj Muki Betser and Col Baruch Bar Lev, whose local knowledge was to prove vital for the raid on Entebbe. Here, a Ugandan trainee pilot, John Etiange, undertakes pre-flight checks of a Fouga Magister under the watchful eye of LtCol Matetyahu Caspi, the Israeli commander of the Uganda Air Force School, at Entebbe Airport on June 1, 1966.

Often portrayed in the Western media as a comic buffoon and a cruel eccentric, Idi Amin was a brutal dictator that dragged his country to wrack and ruin. With 40 children by seven official wives, Amin was much affected by his early life in the colonial British Army, where he rose to the rank of *effendi,* or warrant officer—the highest rank obtainable by a black African. With independence, he became lieutenant in 1961, being promoted to colonel within four years, and to field marshal by 1975. Through his disastrous administration, Uganda became a pariah state that was described by the U.S. Ambassador in 1973 as "racist, erratic, and unpredictable, brutal, inept, bellicose, irrational, ridiculous, and militaristic." (Photo by Getty Images)

civilian construction projects and when Israel refused to write off these debts, Amin turned to Libya and Saudi Arabia for economic aid. As a corollary, they demanded all Israelis be expelled from the country and that Amin embrace the struggle against "Zionism and imperialism," espousing "the right of return of the Palestinian people to their homes and lands." At that time there were some 470 Israeli civil engineers or members of the military mission under the command of Col Baruch "Burka" Bar Lev (a longstanding confidant of Idi Amin). On March 27, 1972, President Amin demanded their expulsion, and by April 8, all of them had left the country. Among the last to depart from Entebbe Airport was Maj Moshe "Muki" Betser; his next military assignment would be a return to the Sayeret Matkal, a move that would be hugely beneficial in the ensuing crisis. Soon after the withdrawals, the Israeli Ambassador's residence at 17 McKinnon Road in Kampala was handed over to the local PLO representative, Haled al-Sid.

As President Amin transformed himself into a devout Muslim, large loans flowed in from Libya and Saudi Arabia. On August 4, 1972, the president gave the entrepreneurial Asian community, mainly Gujarati Indians, just 90 days to leave the country on the grounds that these so-called "brown Jews" were sabotaging the Ugandan economy. All their businesses and accumulated wealth were expropriated by the state. Similarly, all Asians in the Ugandan civil service were dismissed and many positions filled by Palestinians. The Libyans supplied MiG fighters to replace the Fouga Magister aircraft and financed a 300-man Palestinian personal bodyguard for Amin. Despite Arab aid, however, the economy collapsed under the inept and murderous regime. In September 1972, Amin declared the black Jewish community in Uganda, known as the *Abayudaya,* to be illegal and all synagogues were closed. On September 11, President Amin sent a telegram to the United Nations Secretary General, Dr. Kurt Waldheim; in it, he applauded the massacre of Israeli athletes at the Munich Olympic Games and stated that Germany was the most appropriate place for such action because "it was where Hitler had burned more than six million Jews" and that this in itself was because "all of the German people knew that the Israelis are not a people who work for humanity and because of that, they burned them alive and killed them with gas on the soil of Germany."[1] Even as the country slipped into anarchy and its people into starvation, President Idi Amin was made chairman of the Organization of African Unity on July 28, 1975. His term was due to end on July 2, 1976, which would be at the height of the Entebbe hostage crisis.

Day 2: Monday June 28, 1976

During Monday afternoon, the Israeli government learned from a British Broadcasting Corporation (BBC) news reports that Flight 139 had landed at Entebbe, but as yet there were no demands from the hijackers. Later bulletins indicated that the hostages had been moved into the Old Terminal building. As a former commander of Sayeret Matkal, Col Ehud Barak was now the assistant to the Chief of Military Intelligence and responsible for research and Special Forces operations. He immediately set up an ad hoc planning group of the IDF's leading counterterrorism specialists. As the commander of Sayeret Matkal, LtCol Yonatan "Yoni" Netanyahu and his deputy Maj Yiftah Reicher were currently away on exercise at Um Hashiba in the Sinai Desert,

---

1 Controversially, Dr. Waldheim, a former Wehrmacht Intelligence Officer, did not choose to challenge the communication.

Barak summoned their representative, Muki Betser, to the meeting. Thanks to his prior posting, Betser was able to deliver his assessment of the Ugandan troops, highlighting their lack of motivation and their reluctance to fight at night. Despite an absence of orders from government or IDF high command for a military rescue mission, planning began with a close scrutiny of original blueprints for the Old Terminal that had been obtained from the Israeli civil engineering company, Solel Boneh.

Similarly, the Israeli Air Force began informally considering a rescue mission. As the commander of No. 131 "Yellow Bird" Squadron, LtCol Joshua "Shiki" Shani called a meeting of his staff to discuss the hijacking. He recalls: "We did some private planning exercises and learned that the C-130 was the only airplane that could get to Entebbe and carry enough people and equipment. I was sitting with my staff, my two deputies, the chief flight engineer, and the chief navigator. We looked at range, fuel, payload, navigation, weather problems, things that take time to cover. We worked for six hours or so." Since the distance to Entebbe was some 2,200 miles (3,541 km), it was apparent that only the squadron's two KC-130 aerial tanker aircraft had the range to complete a return journey without refueling; even so, this would have to be with a much reduced payload as the supplementary 3,000 Imperial gal stainless-steel fuel tank of each plane was situated in the cargo hold. An ordinary C-130 Hercules could reach Uganda in under eight hours but would then have only one and a half hours of flying time thereafter. Up until March 1972, Hercules transport aircraft of the Israeli Air Force had made regular supply runs to Entebbe for the Israeli military mission in Uganda. The commander of the Israeli Air Force, MajGen Benny Peled, took an immediate interest in their deliberations, and Shiki Shani was able to convince him that his "Yellow Birds" could fly up to 1,000 troops to Entebbe. The major problem of refueling remained, but a number of potential solutions were considered. Thereafter Gen Peled was a strong advocate of the Air Force military solution.

Day 3: Tuesday June 29, 1976

The Israeli government's political inactivity of Monday allowed the French government of President Valery Giscard d'Estaing and Prime Minister Jacques Chirac to conduct negotiations with the hijackers, but as the latter had yet to make any demands, little progress was made. After resting and relaxing overnight in Kampala, the hijackers returned to the Old Terminal at Entebbe on Tuesday morning. That afternoon, Fouad Awad issued a communiqué listing the hijackers' demands, which, at 1530hrs, was broadcast to the world over Uganda Radio. Primarily, 53 terrorists held in five countries were to be released; these comprised 40 in Israel, six in West Germany, five in Kenya, and one each in France and Switzerland. Among the prisoners in Israel were Kozo Okamoto of the Japanese Red Army and Archbishop Hilarion Capucci, the spiritual leader and primate of the Greek Orthodox Church in Jerusalem who had been convicted for smuggling arms for Fatah in his official car. All 40 held in Israel were to be flown to Entebbe aboard an Air France aircraft; the other prisoners were to be transported to Uganda by the nations holding them. After the transfers were complete, the aircraft was to fly them and the hijackers to a safe haven in the Middle East. All negotiations were to be conducted solely between a special French envoy and Hashi Abdallah, Somali Ambassador to Uganda. In addition,

The three principals in the raid on Entebbe are shown during an inspection of military positions on the Golan Heights in December 1975 with (from left to right) Defense Minister Shimon Peres, Prime Minister Yitzhak Rabin, and IDF Chief of Staff Mordechai "Motta" Gur. The latter subsequently wrote a children's book *Azit Hakalba Hatzanhanit,* or "Azit the Paratrooper Dog," and a sequel entitled *Azit b'Entebbe*—"Azit in Entebbe"—that depicted a slight revision of history with Azit parachuting into Entebbe with Yoni and his Special Forces.

the French government was to pay a ransom of U.S. $5 million for the return of the Air France A300 Airbus. A deadline was set for 1400hrs [Israeli time] on Thursday July 1. Failure to comply with the stipulations would result in the deaths of the hostages.

On hearing the demands, Prime Minister Rabin immediately called a further meeting of senior cabinet ministers. With the hostages held some 2,000 miles (3,219 km) away by zealous foreign activists who were seemingly protected by a volatile African dictator, Israel was faced with the very real possibility of having to accede to the terrorists. Nevertheless, Rabin summoned the IDF Chief of Staff, Lt Gen Motta Gur, to determine whether there was any military means of resolving the crisis. Without delay, Gur ordered his adjutant, LtCol Hagai Regev, to instruct the Operations Branch at the Kirya to start making preliminary plans for possible military action. Col Ehud Barak and his Special Forces colleagues were already exploring every feasible option, but nothing specific had yet been agreed when Gur, at the earliest opportunity, arranged a conference with Defense Minister Peres. Among the senior commanders present were Kuti Adam and Benny Peled. Adam was convinced that a military option was necessary. Peled, however, was confident that the Air Force would be capable of delivering 1,200 troops and equipment to Entebbe within a 24-hour period without encountering any resistance by Ugandan air defenses. Despite his certainty, Peled went on to propose a more limited operation using just four Hercules aircraft and a much smaller body of troops—an option preferred by Maj Ido Embar, since there were, in fact, only four operational flight crews trained to land the C-130 at night.

Defense Minister Shimon Peres later recalled the meeting and the confidence exuded by Benny Peled, who, with a straight face, had demanded: "What do you want? That we conquer Entebbe or the whole country?" Peres recounted: "I asked him, 'How many do you need for that?' 'To conquer the whole country I need 1,000 soldiers—to conquer Entebbe maybe 200 or 300 men.' I liked his daring."

As Chief of Staff of the IDF, with ultimate responsibility for the deployment of Israeli forces, Motta Gur remained sceptical about a military option. Intelligence reports relating to where and how the hostages were being held remained vague, and the meeting concluded without any firm decision being made. Throughout the night Barak and his team continued to formulate possible options according to their own particular field of expertise and, by daybreak, emerged with four proposals. The most seriously considered scheme called for a joint operation

In the aftermath of the October War of 1973, the prestige of the IDF plummeted in the national consciousness. It fell further following an appalling terrorist attack on the Netiv Meir School in Ma'alot on May 15, 1974. A rescue mission was conducted by the Sayeret Matkal and the Sayeret Golani into the second story of the building, where the hostages were being held. The firefight lasted a ghastly 12 minutes during which time the screaming students were cut down by automatic weapons fire and exploding hand grenades before all the terrorists were killed. Twenty-two teenagers, mostly girls, died in the carnage, and another 50 were injured. In all 26 people died in the Ma'alot massacre. Here, Golani soldiers rescue the wounded during the course of the operation.

between Shayetet 13 and Sayeret Matkal, with the Special Forces being dropped by parachute from C-130 Hercules aircraft into Lake Victoria. After a covert approach to the shore in Zodiac inflatable boats, the Sayeret Matkal were to advance just over half a mile (.8 km) through crocodile-infested swamp to the Old Terminal, eliminate the terrorists, and then surrender to the Ugandan authorities. The second idea was similar in concept but called for a boat to be hired in Kenya and used to ferry the troops across Lake Victoria to Entebbe Airport to undertake the attack. As the representative of the Paratroop and Infantry Command, LtCol Haim Oren recommended a large-scale parachute drop to capture the whole airport (as originally advocated by Benny Peled to Peres). Finally, Muki Betser suggested flying a civilian aircraft into Entebbe, supposedly carrying the released terrorists, but in fact transporting the rescue force of Sayeret Matkal dressed as Palestinian prisoners. Three out of the four plans were based on the assumption that the Ugandan authorities would be amenable to such rescue attempts and allow everyone to leave, while the fourth would tax the resources of the Israeli Air Force to the full. Moreover, no mission could be successfully implemented without exact knowledge of the airport terminal and where the hostages were kept imprisoned. Muki Betser later recounted how a Mossad operative was tasked with sourcing this vital information:

> We took a Mossad operative, a pilot, whose job was to carry out different photo shoots for them in all kinds of places. He flew from London to Nairobi in Kenya. At Nairobi, he rented a light aeroplane, flew to Entebbe—and then informed the control tower he had a technical malfunction and had to perform some aerial roundabouts in the air[…]The Mossad operative made a couple of rounds and photographed the old terminal. Afterwards he told the control tower that he could not land, went back to Nairobi and sent the photos to Israel.

Astonishingly the Ugandans confirmed their reputation for slack security as they never suspected this was a ruse, despite the hijack drama that was unfolding at the airport. The photographs would provide crucial information to the military planners of the subsequent raid.

The Room of Separation

Meanwhile, for the hostages, Tuesday was another day of fear and apprehension. The dilapidated Old Terminal building, measuring some 65 feet (20 m) by 50 feet (15 m), was now crammed with 257 men, women, and children including the 12 Air France aircrew. Those who had slept on old mattresses lying on the floor suffered from a rash of bites. The heat was stifling, and few had the energy to do anything other than sit listlessly. Most of the hijackers lounged outside in armchairs, shading themselves under awnings from the tropical sun. Permission was needed for any visit to the lavatories, which were soon reeking and overflowing with excrement. Among jokes as to whether it was made with crocodile meat, there was little appetite for the curry and rice served from large tureens. Nevertheless, there was still optimism that the hostages would be released soon, and some were speculating as to how long the flight time would take to Paris. As Sarah Davidson noted in a small, secret diary she was keeping: "A plane will shortly arrive to take us. Everything is now being settled. We'll soon be flying onwards on our family excursion."

Another visit by President Idi Amin was met with mixed emotions by the hostages. Some applauded his speech while others were appalled by the spectacle. One hostage

JUNE 28, 1976

0315hrs: Flight 139 lands at Entebbe International Airport, Uganda.

JUNE 29, 1976

1530hrs: Hijackers issue their demands.

JUNE 29, 1976

1910hrs: Israeli and Jewish hostages separated from the other captives.

later recalled: "I really felt at that moment what fear meant. Amin was something like Hitler. I felt that I was in a world of frightening nightmare, like the concentration camps of World War II." His comparison was soon to become even more prophetic. During the course of the afternoon, Ugandan soldiers began to smash a doorway through a partition wall with sledgehammers. As the hostages waited for their evening meal, Brigitte Kuhlmann began to separate Israelis and Jews from all other nationalities and forced them into the adjoining room. Medical student Moshe Peretz noted in his diary: "1910[hrs]. The terrorists are separating us from the rest in most dramatic fashion. Everyone with an Israeli passport is asked to go out of the main hall into the next one. There is a sense of imminent execution. Women begin to weep." Those chosen for this new humiliation called it the "Room of Separation." It was redolent of the dreaded *Selektzia* ("Selection of the Holocaust"), where inmates were chosen to either live or die. To suffer their own selection process by young German nationals made the ordeal all the more terrifying for the hostages. One concentration camp survivor among the hostages declared: "I felt myself back 32 years when I heard the German orders and saw the waving guns. I imagined the shuffling lines of prisoners and the harsh cries of 'Jews to the right' and I wondered what good is Israel if this can happen today."

Day 4: Wednesday June 30, 1976

MajGen Benny Peled was the commander of the Israeli Air Force during the raid on Entebbe. From the outset he advocated a military operation to rescue the hostages and provided the early impetus that expedited planning and ensured that the Air Force was ready to execute the raid over such a vast distance.

It was also a question troubling the minds of many people in the Israeli government and military. It was the fourth day of the hijack, and despite many hours of deliberation through the night, the four schemes put forward by the planning team met with little enthusiasm when they were presented to Prime Minister Rabin in the morning. As the former Chief of Staff who had led the IDF to victory during the Six Day War, he dismissed them out of hand with the opinion that it would result in Israel's "Bay of Pigs." The IDF was instructed to reassess and develop the options further. Intelligence, however, was still lacking despite the arrival of an Israeli Navy electronic communications monitoring vessel off the coast of East Africa. In addition, any military option would require the intelligence-gathering resources of Mossad, whose agents were still being deployed to Kenya and Uganda, to coordinate local operatives and assess the ground. During the course of the day, a major exercise in the Sinai Desert concluded, releasing a number of officers for immediate return to Tel Aviv, where they were briefed on the hijacking. They included BrigGen Dan Shomron (who, as head of the Paratroop and Infantry Branch, was deputed to command the ground forces of any military assault on Entebbe) and Col Shai Tamari, the second in command of the Special Operations Division of Operations Branch that had the overall responsibility for any raid on Entebbe. Accordingly, he assumed control of the military response to the hijacking from Col Ehud Barak. A team was then dispatched on El Al Flight 535 to Kenya to seek the assistance of the government there to resolve the crisis and augment the intelligence-gathering operation on the ground. Dan Shomron later recounted his view of the original plan to parachute Special Forces into the area:

On Wednesday it was clear that there was a real chance of going with an operation. I flew up and didn't receive any instructions. They updated me that there was a certain scheme to parachute 12 fighters into Lake Victoria and from there they would get onto dinghies, reach the terminal, enter and kill the terrorists, and then we'd see what would happen. I look at the intelligence and don't understand this. There are two points with no answers: the one is the idea to sneak in through the swamps—indeed if someone gets spotted there's a lot of time to kill all the hostages, and then there are these 12 stuck there. The second issue is the question of evacuation. How will an evacuation be done while Idi Amin is not cooperating with us and there are Ugandan soldiers all around the terminal? It looked to me like a dud of a plan.

Nevertheless, since the parachute drop into Lake Victoria remained the primary military option, it was decided to see whether the scheme was feasible with the existing equipment. The first drop from a C-130 into the Mediterranean Sea was unsuccessful when the inflatable boats, released from the designated height, exploded on contact with the water. The second option also seemed increasingly unlikely when the Kenyan government intimated that it would not allow any action against Uganda that was initiated from its soil. Following his meeting with generals Adam and Peled the previous evening, Defense Minister Peres sought the advice of officers that had served in Uganda and were acquainted with President Amin in order to obtain a fuller psychological profile of the unpredictable dictator. In particular, Peres requested the services of a retired officer, Col Baruch "Burka" Bar Lev, the former commander of the Israeli military mission in Uganda and a personal friend of Idi Amin. Over the coming days, Burka Bar Lev made several international phone calls to President Amin, soliciting his personal assistance in the crisis, while playing on his ego with inducements such as a nomination for the Nobel Peace Prize should he orchestrate the release of the hostages. The calls were closely monitored and assessed for any piece of intelligence that Amin might let slip during the conversations. As a result of these discussions, Peres became increasingly convinced that a military solution was necessary to resolve the crisis.

On the political front, the Israeli Cabinet met at 1100hrs, but there was little progress to be gleaned beyond the recent announcement by France and West Germany that they would not release the terrorists held in their custody. Most international observers believed this statement was made for public show and that both governments would ultimately follow the lead set by Israel. The general consensus of the meeting was that the decision whether or not to accede to the hijackers' demands could be delayed, since the deadline was still some 24 hours away. But as yet there was no real alternative, since the IDF had failed to produce a coherent and comprehensive military plan for consideration by the cabinet. Throughout the day, the Israeli Air Force developed its strategy for the air assault on Entebbe, but now the scale of the operation was becoming more limited, with just six aircraft, rather than the 1,200-man paratroop drop as originally advocated by Benny Peled. Both Peled and Kuti Adam were convinced that an air landing by Hercules aircraft was the most feasible military option. One of the major problems of the original concept was how to fly such a large number of unarmed aircraft some 2,000 miles (3,219 km) over a number of hostile countries without detection. Planning now revolved around the use of just four C-130 Hercules aircraft supported by two Boeing 707s, with one dedicated to command and control while the other would be an airborne hospital to treat any wounded. The problem of refueling for the return trip remained unanswered, but possibilities lay in transporting the hostages in a KC-130, which had the fuel capacity to fly there and back, while the other three aircraft of the landing force would need to acquire sufficient fuel for their return from the tanks located at Entebbe.

Following the earlier telephone conversations between Col Burka Bar Lev and President Amin, there was growing unease that Amin was aiding the terrorists, a situation that dramatically altered the military options. Any idea of covertly eliminating the terrorists and then surrendering to the Ugandan authorities became increasingly doubtful, despite a second successful attempt by Shayetet 13 to paradrop Zodiac inflatable boats. From his experience in Uganda, Muki Betser was not unhappy with the demise of the paradrop scheme as "the crocodiles in Lake Victoria are among the largest in the world. The Unit can cope with many things, but battling with crocodiles is not one of them." Accordingly, BrigGen Dan Shomron continued to advocate a larger force to capture Entebbe Airport and prevent intervention by Ugandan troops, in line with Peled's original proposal. At 2100hrs, Shomron convened a planning session at his headquarters, where a rough operational concept was put together. It proposed landing a rescue force drawn from Sayeret Matkal on the main runway that would then proceed to the Old Terminal and eliminate the terrorists. Thereafter more aircraft would land large numbers of paratroops with the task of occupying the entire airport and guarding against any Ugandan counterattacks while the hostages were being evacuated. Further high-level meetings were held with Defense Minister Peres and Prime Minister Rabin, but the intractable problem of lack of intelligence concerning the exact whereabouts of the hostages remained unresolved.

The Entebbe Hilton

For the hostages on their third day of imprisonment at Entebbe, the conditions inside the Old Terminal were rapidly deteriorating, leading to ironic comments about the "Entebbe Hilton." Following a request to President Idi Amin, towels and blankets had been provided the previous day (although blankets were hardly necessary in the sweltering heat), and new mattresses helped alleviate the problem with bed bugs. Fear and apprehension still stalked the Jewish hostages confined in the "Room of Separation." As Sarah Davidson noted in her diary:

> All these years I didn't comprehend what the Holocaust meant. Year after year I read over and over again what is published on the subject and I see the films and I listen again to the dreadful testimonies. And I don't understand. Why did the Jews file quietly and abjectly into the gas chambers? Why did they go like sheep led to the slaughter, when they already had nothing left to lose? I needed this nightmare at Entebbe to help me understand. Now, only now, I understand. It's easy to deceive people who so much want to live.

That afternoon, 47 gentile hostages, mainly French nationals, were placed on an aircraft and flown to Orly Airport in Paris as a goodwill gesture by the self-professed "savior" of the unfortunate captives, President Idi Amin. They arrived at Orly to be welcomed by the French Foreign Minister, Jean Sauvagnargues, and their relieved and delighted families. As soon as the IDF learned that some of the hostages were being released, former Sayeret Matkal deputy commander, LtCol Amiram Levine was sent to Paris to direct the military intelligence gathering effort for any rescue attempt. Levine had to work very discreetly, as Prime Minister Rabin had earlier sent his special advisor on terrorism, Gen Rehavam "Gandhi" Zeevi, to Europe to coordinate any political negotiations with the French should an exchange of terrorists for hostages become necessary. If Zeevi were to see Levine in Paris, he would immediately realize that a military operation was being planned, which could well affect his judgement in any negotiations. The overall responsibility for acquiring and collating information from all sources lay with the Director of Military Intelligence, MajGen Shlomo Gazit. Only when he was completely satisfied that there was sufficient, accurate, and timely intelligence in place could a military operation be recommended to the Chief of Staff, and through him to the political leadership.[2]

---

2 For a fuller account of the complexities behind the political and operational planning of the Entebbe raid, see the monograph by MajGen Shlomo Gazit published in *International Security* Vol. 6 No. 1 Summer 1981 by the President and Fellows of Harvard College and the Massachusetts Institute of Technology.

During the course of the night, several of the families were visited at their homes by members of the French Security Services and representatives from the Israeli embassy, including Levine. All the hostages were willing to pass on whatever information they could about the conditions under which they had been held in Uganda. The recollections of a former French military officer were of vital importance. For three days, he had been making mental notes about every aspect of the hijackers, their weapons, the Ugandan guards, and the daily routine. Realizing immediately that the Israelis were planning a rescue mission, his prodigious memory provided a wealth of intelligence that had been completely lacking to date. In particular, he was able to identify key points on blueprints of the airport buildings, indicating the number of hostages, as well as the number of terrorists on the ground. Moreover, he was able to confirm that neither the hostage-takers nor the Ugandan forces expected a military response from the IDF and were accordingly lax in their arrangements.

JUNE 30, 1976

2100hrs: BrigGen Dan Shomron convenes operational planning meeting.

Day 5: Thursday July 1, 1976

Throughout the crisis, LtCol Yoni Netanyahu, the commander of Sayeret Matkal, had been kept informed of developments. Although he had been fully occupied all week on a prearranged military exercise in Sinai, he had remained in contact with the planning staff to ensure that The Unit would be involved in any military option. Following telephone calls from Muki Betser during the night informing him that military intervention was now under serious consideration, an exhausted Netanyahu flew back during the morning to meet up with his men at Ramat Gan and be briefed by Betser. By now three of the four original schemes had been eliminated, leaving what was termed the "IDF Option" of employing C-130 Hercules transport aircraft to carry as yet an undetermined commando force to Entebbe Airport. The actual

LIEUTENANT COLONEL YONATAN NETANYAHU

He joined the IDF in 1964 and elected to join the paratroops. During the Six Day War of 1967, he fought in both the Sinai and on the Golan Heights, where he was seriously injured in the elbow by a gunshot wound. During the early 1970s, he was selected for the Sayeret Matkal and participated in several significant missions, including Operations *Crate 3* and *Springtime of Youth*. In the October War of 1973, he again fought on the Golan Heights and was awarded the Medal of Distinguished Service—the IDF's third highest military decoration for an act of exemplary bravery in the line of duty. Thereafter, he temporarily transferred to the Israeli Armored Corps following their appalling casualty rate among officers during the October War. He was given command of the 188th Barak Armored Brigade that had been completely shattered during the defense of the Golan Heights. In June 1975, Yoni Netenyahu returned to Sayeret Matkal as its commanding officer. He was the only IDF fatality during Operation *Thunderbolt*, which was re-named Operation *Yonatan* in his honor. Just prior to his death, he wrote: "The basic assumption in our work is to prepare in the best possible fashion, so that we may stand quietly on the Day of Judgement, when it comes, in the knowledge that we did everything we could in the time that we had." And that is certainly what Yoni did during his brief life of 30 years.

method of eliminating the hijackers and releasing the hostages had still to be resolved. Netanyahu and The Unit began to address the problems. The same morning, Israeli newspapers were published with "SELEKTZIA" as a banner headline. Nothing was guaranteed to inflame Israeli public opinion more. As LtCol Joshua Shani commented: "We said this can't be happening to us. It's 1976 in a free country. The Germans are doing the same thing again. It made me very angry..."

For the families of the hostages, it made the situation even more unbearable. A Committee of Relatives had been formed soon after the crisis began to liaise with the government and to keep families abreast of developments. Fears had escalated when the original 47 hostages were released, but when the remaining 101 gentiles were also allowed to leave Entebbe on board an Air France aircraft on Thursday morning, relatives were incensed.

When the captain of Flight 139, Michel Bacos, had been informed about the release on Wednesday evening, he had called together his crew: "I told them our duty is to stay with the passengers until the end no matter what happens." All of them, down to the most junior flight attendant, agreed to stay with the remaining hostages. When it came to boarding, a French nun volunteered to stay behind in place of one of the elderly Jewish prisoners, but she was peremptorily refused and forced onto the aircraft. Now only 94 Jews remained, almost all of them Israelis, together with the 12 Air France crew. The "selection" was complete and the families were outraged. They besieged the prime minister's office in force, insisting that the hijackers demands be met despite Israel's policy of not negotiating with terrorists. As one distraught mother stated: "We knew it was a principle and that Israel served the world as an example of no surrender to terrorists but all this was being said about our child and we wanted our child back alive and not principles…"

The pressure on Prime Minister Yitzhak Rabin was intense. The deadline of 1400hrs was looming. An early-morning conversation with Chief of Staff Motta Gur indicated that the IDF needed more intelligence and, critically, more time to formulate a viable military plan. At 0900hrs, all 18 cabinet ministers met with the prime minister. After a preliminary discussion, Rabin left the meeting to consult with the Knesset Foreign Affairs and Security Committee. He informed them of the government's intention to request the French Foreign Ministry negotiate directly with the Somalian Ambassador in Kampala for an exchange of terrorists for hostages. Returning to the cabinet room, Prime Minister Rabin called for a vote, insisting that each minister should vote for or against the proposal of negotiation, but that there could be no avoidance of responsibility by abstention. The vote was unanimously in favor of negotiation. Rabin then conferred with the leader of the Likud opposition, Menachem Begin, who had been kept informed about the situation as it had unfolded, and who likewise agreed to the proposal. The decision reached the hijackers with just 90 minutes remaining to the deadline. The response was swift. In a telephone conversation to Burka Bar Lev, Idi Amin counselled him to listen to an announcement on Radio Uganda at 1400hrs. It was soon broadcast around the world: "From the BBC World Service. This is London. Ashley Hodgson with the news. The deadline at Entebbe Airport for compliance with the hijackers' demands has been extended until 1100hrs Greenwich Mean Time (GMT) on Sunday." Given that the Israeli government had capitulated to the hijackers' demands, Amin had arranged with the PFLP to extend the exchange deadline until 1400hrs local time on Sunday July 4. In his capacity as chairman of the Organization of African Unity, Amin would be absent during the interim, in Mauritius; he would not wish to miss his hour of glory on the world stage should the exchange take place while he was away.

THE ISRAELI PLANS

Operation *Stanley*

The IDF needed time to prepare. Every hour allowed the plans of the various IDF branches, including the Air Force, paratroopers, and The Unit, to proceed apace. Maj Ido Embar continued his complex calculations of fuel capacities and range versus payload for the Hercules aircraft. He also tried to persuade the higher command that just four C-130 Hercules would suffice. He argued that even this number would require at least eight fully qualified pilots, as well as the most experienced navigators, to find a darkened runway in an unfamiliar airport with precision timing. The Unit was also of the firm conviction that the assault teams should be as compact as possible for maximum tactical control. Accordingly, both the Air Force and The Unit were in agreement as to the scale of the air assault to capture Entebbe Airport. One fundamental question remained however—how to get The Unit assault team from the main runway to the Old Terminal without detection, a distance of 1 mile (1.6 km), in an international airport that, according to the latest intelligence reports, was guarded by hundreds of Ugandan soldiers. The problem was resolved by Muki Betser, thanks to his experience with the Ugandan Army and the political elite. He knew that all senior Ugandan officers and politicians were driven in Mercedes-Benz motorcars, a veritable icon of corruption and repression in a host of African countries, and to which soldiers showed due deference. Idi Amin himself was known to travel in a motorcade comprising a large black Mercedes-Benz with outriders and escorts. Betser proposed replicating this scenario, cramming a Mercedes-Benz limousine with Unit fighters and providing an escort of two Land Rovers.

MajGen Kuti Adam was the IDF Chief of Operations in 1976 and was a critical force in the planning and execution of the Entebbe raid as he was in the Boeing 707 command and control aircraft circling above the airport and coordinating Operation *Thunderbolt*. General Adam died in combat in the assault on Beaufort Castle during the invasion of Lebanon in 1982: he is the highest-ranking member of the IDF to be killed in action.

This inspired idea was readily accepted, but it necessitated finding a motorcar in short order. Mossad managed to source a Mercedes from a car dealership that had links to the intelligence organization, but, unfortunately, it was white in color and a repaint would have to be arranged. It was yet another emergency remedy. Some soldiers expressed unease with the rushed, almost amateurish air to the plans. Sayeret Matkal was used to weeks of careful planning with the acquisition of specialized equipment wherever necessary for its operations beyond Israel's borders. The situation now called for the timescale to be compressed into a matter of days. Any disquiet was compounded by the fact that on numerous occasions, Sayeret Matkal had spent much time and effort preparing for various operations, only for them to be aborted at the last moment. Many felt that this venture was more fanciful than most and likely to be canceled in due course. The operation was even given the fanciful title Operation *Stanley*, named after the African explorer. By now, however, intelligence reports were pouring in from several quarters, not least of which were those from the debriefings of the newly released hostages. Mossad agents in East Africa were also able to furnish the order of battle of the Ugandan Army and its current dispositions, indicating that almost half of its 21,000 troops were

normally based between Entebbe and the capital Kampala just 22 miles (35 km) away. This was a formidable force by any measure.

To forestall their intervention, it was decided to include four. M38A1C Jeeps carrying pintle-mounted machine guns and light antitank weapons in two of the C-130 Hercules aircraft. The four vehicles and their crews were under the command of Maj Shaul Mofaz, subsequently to become Chief of Staff of the IDF and Defense Minister. Their role was to provide heavier firepower in support of The Unit, once it had attacked the Old Terminal, against any possible Ugandan counterattacks. BrigGen Dan Shomron assigned a force drawn from the 35th Parachute Brigade, under the command of Col Matan Vilnai, to capture the New Terminal, control tower, and the aviation fuel tanks. Mindful of its distinguished military record, Shomron also ordered members of the Sayeret Golani (of the famous Golani Infantry Brigade) under the command of Col Uri Sagie, to act as a blocking force, to protect the vulnerable C-130 aircraft on the ground and to assist in the evacuation of the hostages.

EHUD BARAK

He was one of the most influential commanders of Sayeret Matkal at the time that "The Unit," as it is colloquially known, was assuming more responsibility for counterterrorism operations. He famously led Operation *Springtime of Youth* to assassinate PLO leaders living in Beirut on the night of April 9/10, 1973, when the raiding force was landed on the beaches of Beirut from Zodiac boats of Shayetet 13 and from there into the city by cars driven by Mossad agents. All the raiders were disguised as civilian tourists with several members dressed as women whose ample bosoms concealed hand grenades and explosive charges. Major Moshe "Muki" Betser was partnered with his commanding officer, Ehud Barak, who sported a brunette wig so that they appeared to be a courting couple as they approached the apartment block on the Rue Verdun where the PLO leaders lived; also assigned to Muki Betser's assault team was Captain Yonathan "Yoni" Netanyahu. All the targets were eliminated, but a heavy firefight erupted on the Rue Verdun as The Unit made its withdrawal. Muki Betser later recounted: "I ran down the hall to the stairs, leaping from landing to landing, on our way to the street, where the firefight grew louder. Out the front door, I ducked into the shadow of a tree, scanning the intersection just as a burning Lebanese police Land Rover rolled through the intersection. Straight ahead, Amiram Levine in a blonde wig looked like a crazed dancer in the middle of the intersection, his tiny powerful body swinging his Uzi back and forth from target to target. To my right Ehud [Barak] stood in the middle of the intersection doing the same. I added my own fire at the Land Rover, giving Amiram cover for him to run toward me. The Land Rover crashed to a halt against a building. But a second vehicle, a jeep full of reinforcements, came screeching into the box of fire we created at the intersection. Bursts of gunfire knocked the four passengers out of the vehicle, as our fire strafed the jeep." By the application of superior firepower, The Unit was able to withdraw to the beaches without further casualties from where they were exfiltrated by Shayetet 13. Operation *Springtime of Youth* had achieved all its aims and it came as a fearful shock to the PLO leadership as they realized they were no longer safe even in the heart of Beirut, since Yasser Arafat often used the buildings that The Unit attacked as well. A Lebanese newspaper reported the raid in the most lurid terms: "...two beautiful she-devils, a blonde and a brunette, who fought off the police and army like dervishes with machine guns." Here, the "dervish" poses with his Uzi 9mm submachine gun with an unidentified attachment: The Unit often advised Israel Military Industries in weapons development, particularly the Mini-Uzi for covert operations. Ehud Barak was superseded as commander of Sayeret Matkal in June 1976 by LtCol Yoni Netanyahu. As one of the most decorated officers of the IDF, Ehud Barak later became Prime Minister of Israel.

At 1600hrs MajGen Kuti Adam called Dan Shomron to ask whether an operational plan now existed. When Shomron answered in the affirmative he was instructed to outline the operation directly to Shimon Peres and his aides. Shomron later recounted how the plan was presented and received:

> I didn't make a [formal] presentation—not to the Chief of Staff and not to anyone. I went directly to Peres. I confirmed that on the night between Saturday and Sunday we carry out the operation. After I present the plan, Peres asks every one of those present: "what chance do you give to this? How many casualties do you think there will be? Do you recommend the execution of this plan?" Most of them didn't want to answer. Kuti gave it a 50 percent chance. The commander of the Air Force, Benny Peled, proposed parachuting a full brigade and I replied that before the first paratrooper lands in the country all the hostages will be killed.

At this critical gathering, there were still many issues to be resolved before the plan could be presented to the cabinet for approval. As Dan Shomron later explained:

> When Peres turned to Motta Gur [the IDF Chief of Staff], he replied to him: "I'll answer you in a meeting of four eyes [privately]" and I knew that he was very scared with the memory of the terrorist attack on Ma'alot. I understand him. Peres saw that they were not altogether with him and he wanted support, so he asked that I make the presentation again and say what I think. Three times in this deliberation [meeting] on Thursday, I presented and explained why the plan was feasible…He [Peres] asked how many casualties there would be and I said that inasmuch as there would be shooting there, there could possibly be three, four or five killed. I was not mistaken…They said the plan was brilliant, but the risks were great.

Finally Defense Minister Shimon Peres approved the military operation, and overall coordination of the detailed planning was assigned to the Chief of Operations, Col Shai Tamari. He was to report to Chief of Staff Gur, who, prior to the plan's submission to cabinet, had still to be convinced of its feasibility. With Dan Shomron appointed as ground commander and the composition of the assault force now decided, the IDF computer in the Kirya, which generates random names for military operations, came up with the suggested operation name of *Wave of Ash*.

Day 6: Friday July 2, 1976

This unimaginative title for such a daring Special Forces mission did not find favor, and the more dramatic Operation *Thunderbolt* was substituted. At 0100hrs, Motta Gur phoned Shimon Peres and reported that the military plan to rescue the hostages was now ready. During the night, Kuti Adam ordered the construction of a full-scale

An aerial view of the passenger terminal shows the building in its heyday but before the extension was built at the right-hand end. Such photographs were of prime importance during the planning phase of Operation *Thunderbolt*. (Photo by Malcolm Dunstan)

JULY 01, 1976

1600hrs: BrigGen Shomron confirms operational plan and presents it to Shimon Peres.

model of the Old Terminal at Entebbe, based on the available blueprints and photographs. Made up of wooden posts and hessian screens to replicate the building layout, it was erected at the Sayeret Matkal base where rehearsals could take place. However, the Mercedes-Benz was not yet ready. Procured by Mossad, it was a diesel automatic D220 Lang (long wheelbase model) that had been used as a taxi. Being white in color, it was currently unsuitable as a substitute for the black limousine of President Amin. Amitzur Kafri, who was in charge of The Unit's special military equipment and arms, was tasked with preparing the vehicle together with Danny Dagan, The Unit's automotive specialist. Kafri later recounted his rather low opinion of the vehicle in question:

> It was a lousy, stupid car that didn't work and it was white. We took it back to The Unit and this guy Razal [the company mechanic] rebuilt it from scratch, painted it black and made it a really good car. If we had believed the mission was really going to happen, we could have gone to a proper Mercedes dealer and bought some new tires. Instead, we went to a friend's tire shop in Jaffa at 0100hrs to replace the four bald tires. He didn't know why and I think we might still owe him money. A guy named Roded from Kibbutz Ma'agan Michael made the Ugandan flag and a [false] licence plate.

His colleague Danny Dagan even undertook the deal for the new tires by signing a note on the back of a napkin from a local restaurant, promising to pay the garage owner within one week.

Certainly, among the soldiers at least, there was still some doubt as to whether the raid would take place or not. Moreover, not all members of The Unit were even aware of the proposed operation until they reported for duty that Friday morning.

> When I arrived at 0800hrs on Friday, I was shocked. Everyone was looking for ammunition like we were going to war. The paratroopers and Golani were gathering, too, like it was D-Day. My commander told me that the IDF was planning a rescue mission, with our unit as the spearhead and our team the tip. I understood the situation was very dangerous. (1st Sgt Amir Ofer)

Vital to the operation was the provision of extensive medical facilities to treat the expected level of casualties, anticipated to be as high as 33 percent and perhaps even more. Col Dr. Efrain Sneh was the Chief of Medical Services, and his immediate thoughts were to plan for the absolute worst-case scenario. Sneh was well aware that the immediate response of the terrorists to an assault would be to kill as many hostages as possible. The success of the operation hinged upon its utter secrecy, but it would be compromised if it became public knowledge that a large amount of blood and plasma had been sourced from the national blood bank. Consequently, word went out that a crisis was developing on the northern border with Lebanon to provide a credible cover story.

At 0830hrs, three C-130 Hercules *Karnaf* (Israeli Air Force name for the C-130, meaning "Rhinoceros" in Hebrew) aircraft were made available to take part in the rehearsals for the raid. Members of The Unit and the Karnaf aircrews repeatedly practiced unshackling and disembarking the vehicles so that precious seconds could be shaved off the unloading time. Throughout the day, Yoni Netanyahu, Muki Betser, and the other officers of The Unit refined the plan; every detail was scrutinized and reassessed until there was no doubt in anyone's mind as to their specific role at any given moment of the raid. Similarly, the paratroops and Golani soldiers honed their

plans for occupying the airport and its various buildings, while the Air Force rigorously prepared the seven aircraft assigned to the mission. Five Hercules in total were made ready, four for the raid itself and one to be held in reserve. Two Boeing 707s would also be employed, one acting as the airborne control center and the other as an airborne medical facility with two integral operating theaters. Primarily, the Air Force needed more up-to-date intelligence on whether any changes had been made to the runways and other airport installations and if any antiaircraft measures had been introduced at the airport or its approaches. Any information regarding standard operating procedures for the runway lights, radar coverage, and access to an international airport was assiduously sought by Israeli intelligence agents, while El Al crews engaged in casual conversations with other airline pilots around the world to tap their knowledge of Entebbe Airport. All data was processed through MajGen Shlomo Gazit's Military Intelligence Directorate and disseminated to the relevant parties strictly as necessary.

Earlier that morning Motta Gur, Kuti Adam, and MajGen Yitzhak "Kaka" Hofi, the chief of Mossad and a keen advocate of a rescue mission, met with Shimon Peres to finalize the operational concept of the mission. In his capacity as IDF Chief of Staff, Gen Motta Gur personally presented the plan to Prime Minister Yitzhak Rabin and Foreign Minister Yigal Allon at 1030hrs. Rabin felt some unease regarding a few aspects, especially the proposal to refuel at Entebbe Airport. He preferred the aircraft should fly on to Nairobi to refuel, even if they were unable to obtain prior permission from the Kenyan authorities, and that in the meantime, further diplomatic efforts should be made to gain that country's cooperation. Even so, Rabin reminded them that the cabinet decision to negotiate with the terrorists was still binding and, although planning could continue, no permission would yet be given for the military option. Ehud Barak was immediately dispatched to Kenya, where he met secretly with senior government figures including the Kenyan Chief of Police Bryn Davies, the Chief of the GSU Geoffrey Karithi, and former British SAS officer Bruce Mackenzie (who acted as a security advisor to President Jomo Kenyatta, with whom the final decision regarding landing rights rested). Central to this decision was the ruling by Attorney General Charles Njojo as to his interpretation of Kenyan civil aviation laws. The departure of Ehud Barak to Kenya overcame a niggling problem in the chain of command. As he had led many Special Forces missions over the years, with the result that he was the most decorated officer in the IDF, Barak had been selected to lead the Sayeret Matkal in the proposed assault against the Old Terminal at Entebbe, inpreference to Yoni Netanyahu. Now, Netanyahu was able to formulate and implement his own plans without hindrance or interference.

One of the lessons of the October War of 1973 was the lack of strategic airlift in the Israeli Air Force to carry vital supplies from the United States, such as electronic countermeasures against the devastating SA-6 antiaircraft missile system. Accordingly, five surplus Boeing 707-320B aircraft were transferred from the Israeli national airline El Al to the Air Force. Over the years, these have been configured as general cargo, command, and communications and as an aerial refueling platform as shown here refueling an F-15 during a demonstration on Air Force Day. During the raid on Entebbe, two Boeings were employed with one in the command and communications role carrying Generals Adam and Peled with their staff as the aircraft circled above Entebbe Airport to control the operation and relay information back to Tel Aviv. The other was configured as a mobile field hospital that flew directly to Nairobi Airport, where it set up in the expectation of heavy casualties.

As GOC of the Paratroop and Infantry Command, BrigGen Dan Shomron was the overall ground commander of Operation *Thunderbolt*. His calm authority throughout the entire planning phase was notable, such as his insistence that various of the elite formations of the IDF were called upon to undertake the raid on Entebbe, thus ensuring that no single unit gained all the glory or, indeed, opprobrium in the case of failure. Dan Shomron subsequently became the 13th IDF Chief of Staff.

Operation *Thunderbolt*—The Plan

The plan was presented to Dan Shomron at 1200hrs together with those of the other assault units of the Sayeret Tzanhanim and the Sayeret Golani, and those of the Karnaf aircrew of the Yellow Bird Squadron. The whole operation was based on the element of surprise. Without it, the remaining 106 hostages could be massacred within moments by automatic fire, hand grenades, and any explosives that may have been placed around the building. The latter remained a serious concern to the last, even though the released Frenchman had already indicated that as the Ugandan soldiers were quartered on the floor above the hostages, this was unlikely.

As part of the airborne task force the two Boeing 707 aircraft would be disguised in El Al livery. The one acting as an airborne command center would oversee the operation and relay communications from the ground back to Tel Aviv. The second Boeing, configured as a field hospital, would proceed directly to Nairobi Airport in Kenya and await any casualties. The lead C-130 Hercules was to be flown by LtCol Joshua Shani together with a second pilot and two navigators. This aircraft was to land first and disgorge the Mercedes-Benz, two Land Rover escorts, and 29 men of The Unit assault force including LtCol Yoni Netanyahu. In addition, it would carry 52 paratroops of Sayeret Tzanhanim, as well as BrigGen Dan Shomron and part of his command group. Ten of the paratroops were tasked with laying portable landing lights alongside the runway to guide in the following aircraft in case the main airstrip lights were extinguished. The second Karnaf was to be piloted by LtCol Nathan "Nati" Dvir. It would transport two M38A1C armed jeeps and men of Sayeret Golani together with Dan Shomron's M38A1C communications jeep, the remainder of his command group, and an additional 17 paratroops. Maj Arieh Oz would fly the third C-130, carrying the other two jeeps and their crews, along with 30 men of Sayeret Golani and another vehicle. The final Karnaf, piloted by Maj Amnon Halivni, would be tasked with extracting the hostages. For the mission it would carry two Peugeot 404 pickup trucks, one of which would be loaded with a portable fuel pump in case the airport pumps were out of commission, together with an Israeli Air Force ten-man refueling crew. The second pickup was to transport the dead and injured. In addition there was a ten-man medical team to treat the wounded and another 20 Golani soldiers to guard the aircraft on the ground.

Despite the shortage of time and the lack of full intelligence, the plan was coherent and militarily feasible. It was, however, totally dependent on the ability of the Israeli Air Force to deliver the Special Forces units with absolute precision into an international airport, without detection, in the middle of the night. It was a tall order by any standards. As with any Special Forces mission, a number of contingency plans had to be put in place in case of complication or even disaster. The fundamental objective was to save the hostages and fly them to freedom. The principal problem for the Air Force planners still remained: the necessity to refuel the aircraft for the return journey. Refueling at Entebbe Airport would have been time consuming and dangerous even if the hostage aircraft was given priority. The alternative proposal, to go on to Nairobi, had the potential to trigger an international incident if the Kenyan government refused permission to land; for then, in order to avoid being stranded in Uganda, the aircraft would have to infringe Kenyan air space and risk being shot down as intruders—a catastrophe if one of them happened to be carrying the 106 hostages.

As the Israeli security regulations do not allow the full facts of the Entebbe raid to be known, what follows is purely speculative, but in the view of the author, fully indicative of the contingency planning necessary in such a Special Forces mission. Israeli sources do reveal that there was a fifth C-130 assigned to the air armada as a

One of the early successes for the Sayeret Matkal in its counterterrorism role was the rescuing of the passengers on a Sabena Boeing 707-329 airliner hijacked by Black September on a flight from Brussels to Tel Aviv on May 8, 1972. After landing at Lod Airport in Tel Aviv, several mechanics in white overalls carrying toolboxes approached to service the aircraft. They were actually members of Sayeret Matkal, and as they burst into the aircraft, they retrieved their weapons from the toolboxes and disabled the hijackers, killing two and wounding the other. Of the 101 passengers, all survived except one woman who jumped up in panic and was shot through the head and fell mortally wounded. The assault lasted just 90 seconds. Here, Ehud Barak with a pistol in his hand stands over the body of a hijacker as the bewildered passengers disembark after the rescue operation; the other member of Sayeret Matkal in the white overalls is Danny Yotam.

reserve aircraft, but this hardly rings true. Any number of other Hercules could be held on stand-by, so it is assumed that this particular aircraft had a specific role. It is known that the Israeli Air Force had two KC-130 tanker aircraft at the time. In all probability, one of these planes accompanied the other four Hercules to Kenya but made a clandestine landing on the vast dry lake bed of the Chalbi Desert to the west of Marsabit in northern Kenya (where it is possible to accommodate five C-130s). It is less than one-hour's flying time from Entebbe and therefore within the endurance range of the raiders. Since the safety of the hostages would take precedence above all else, their aircraft could have been flown there and given enough fuel from the KC-130 to allow it to return to Israel. The remaining fuel, theoretically sufficient for one more Karnaf, would have been used to fly the fighting forces home and any equipment left behind destroyed. In the very worst-case scenario with all four aircraft destroyed on the ground, the four armed jeeps could top and tail a convoy of requisitioned vehicles to allow the IDF soldiers to fight their way through the 120 miles (193 km) of Ugandan territory to the Kenyan border. In the event such measures were unnecessary, but contingency planning is always undertaken to meet any number of possible emergencies and problems of varying magnitude.[3]

Throughout Friday, the various units continued their frenetic preparations of aircraft, vehicles, weapons, and equipment. Although some still doubted that permission would be granted for Operation *Thunderbolt*, the awful realization of the enormity of the mission began to dawn on the principal protagonists in the crisis, particularly for LtCol Joshua Shani and LtCol Yoni Netanyahu. As the pilot of the lead aircraft, Shani later recalled the moment when Rabin tasked him to ensure the success of his part of the mission:

> In one of our discussions, Yitzhak Rabin told me "It is your responsibility to fly precisely, covertly and on time." So the prime minister of my country put all the weight and the responsibility for this mission on my shoulders and it was a very heavy load. My fear was not of being killed. It was of not succeeding and then the whole story would be one of total disaster.

The risks were indeed enormous, not least because Israel had not yet fully recovered from the shock of the 1973 Yom Kippur War, and in many ways the morale of the

---

3 This conclusion is supported both by the available information and current Special Forces aircrews of the RAF, as well as the USMC who were consulted by the author in the preparation of this volume.

country had significantly deteriorated since then. The loss of the hostages together with Israel's elite forces would be a devastating blow to the very spirit of the nation

It was a fear weighing on the mind of IDF Chief of Staff Gen Motta Gur as well. He was still not convinced that all the elements for the mission were in place, particularly the ability of the C-130 aircraft to land in total darkness. He insisted on seeing a demonstration of a night landing, but before darkness fell, he first witnessed a full rehearsal of the operation, including an assault on the mock-up of the Old Terminal. It was hardly a spectacular success. The Mercedes-Benz refused to start, so the Land Rover behind simply pushed it out of the aircraft. "There was a glitch," recalls Amitzur Kafri. "The Mercedes was the first car to leave the Hercules and it didn't start well. Being an automatic car, there is no way to start it up by pushing like you can a shift car. We were afraid something was going to go really wrong, so we decided during the real thing to turn on the car five or ten minutes before landing." A duplicate starter motor was also installed to ensure greater reliability. Amir Ofer recounts: "The dry run was completely unrealistic. In a real rehearsal you should take a flight of eight hours to see how you function and storm a 'real' building. We just hung some fabric to imitate the first-floor terminal. We didn't even shoot. God knows why Motta Gur was happy with the dry run and approved the mission." Col Matan Vilnai took a more phlegmatic view: "Friday evening we had the only rehearsal. It was a very bad one. But in order to have a good operation you need to have a bad rehearsal before it—according to my experience." However, Motta Gur was happy enough and left to fly south with Joshua Shani to undertake a night landing at Ofira Air Base near Sharm el Sheikh on the Red Sea. After the rehearsal, the soldiers were ordered to check every weapon on the firing range, situated only 330–545 yards (302–498 m) from a kibbutz, despite the fact that it was now the Sabbath. On hearing the noise, the nearby inhabitants were outraged and complained to the authorities that the soldiers were breaking the agreed rule of only using pistols on the day of worship. Later, once the truth was revealed, they filled the base with flowers in gratitude for the soldiers' actions.

Throughout the afternoon, Joshua Shani had been practicing blind landings at Ofira Air Base with the C-130's Adverse Weather Aerial Delivery System (AWADS) radar, but with featureless desert around the airstrip it was no easy task. After several trial runs, Shani returned to Lod Airport to pick up generals Gur and Peled for the real demonstration. On flying back to Ofira that night, Shani found the air base in total darkness following orders from Motta Gur for a complete blackout. On his first approach, the radar was unable to give any indication of the runway below; the only discernible object was the chain-link fence that ran parallel to the airstrip. The Hercules' approach fell short, and Shani had to pull up and go round again. As a pilot, Benny Peled realized something was wrong but chose to remain silent. The

During the October War of 1973, the Israeli Air Force received 12 former USAF C-130E Hercules under Operation *Nickel Grass* or Operation *Manof* to the Israelis; *Manof* meaning "crane" in Hebrew. These aircraft, together with the two C-130H models of No. 120 Squadron, were formed into a new Hercules squadron—No. 131 "Ha'Tzipor Ha'Tzehuba" or "Yellow Bird." All these aircraft were subsequently upgraded with new engines and avionics to H-model standard. In the days prior to the raid, the assault force undertook several practice runs in order to speed up the disembarkation of men and vehicles.

This paratrooper (**1**) belongs to the Sayeret Tzanhanim. This elite reconnaissance unit drew its personnel from across the IDF, including the 55th and 35th Parachute Brigades, whose insignia (**2**) and (**3**), respectively, are illustrated here. He is wearing the standard olive green IDF uniform and the new Israeli-designed webbing that saw its combat debut in Operation *Thunderbolt*. He is armed with a folding-stock 5.56mm Galil ARM rifle that had also been recently introduced into service with elite units of the IDF. On his back, he is carrying HE rifle grenades for the Galil. In his left hand are two emergency landing lights that he is about to place along the side of the main runway to guide in following aircraft.

This Sayeret Matkal soldier (**4**) is wearing the Ugandan Army paratrooper uniform. Manufactured in Israel, there were still sufficient stocks available for the Sayeret Matkal team. He is armed with an AK-47 assault rifle with double magazines taped together and an aiming light above the receiver to allow accurate shooting in the dark. Attached to his webbing belt is a loudhailer to shout instructions to the hostages and in his trouser pocket is a field cap with white band for mutual recognition, but most of the troops forgot to wear them in the excitement.

The four Hercules aircraft of No. 131 "Yellow Bird" Squadron that landed at Entebbe during Operation *Thunderbolt* were 4X-FBA/102, 4X-FBB/106, 4X-FBQ/420, and 4X-FBT/435. To this day, they carry this squadron insignia and logo (**5**) on the side of their fuselages.

second attempt was more successful as the Karnaf skimmed the runway before pulling up and returning to Lod Airport, with the congratulations of the IDF Chief of Staff ringing in the ears of the aircrew.

Motta Gur had a final consultation with all the senior officers assigned to Operation *Thunderbolt* in the early hours of Saturday July 3. During the 30-minute meeting, BrigGen Dan Shomron emphasized that the whole mission hinged on the first Karnaf landing at Entebbe Airport undetected. With that fundamental proviso, Yoni Netanyahu was asked his opinion of whether a successful outcome was possible. He replied simply but confidently: "It can be done." After days of doubt, the IDF Chief of Staff was finally convinced.

Day 7: Saturday July 3, 1976

Cabinet Approval for the Operation

In Israel the Sabbath had dawned bright and sunny. The raiders were ready, grabbing last-minute items of equipment and whatever rest they could before the coming ordeal. It was now the responsibility of the political establishment to authorize Operation *Thunderbolt*. The final, awful sanction lay with the prime minister and the cabinet. If the mission failed, many lives would be lost and Israeli military prestige irreparably damaged, inevitably leading to the government's fall. Failure to act militarily meant the only alternative would be to surrender to the terrorists' demands, anathema to official Israeli policy. The previous day, Prime Minister Yitzhak Rabin had begun to canvas support for the military operation, including endorsement by Minister of Justice Haim Zadok as to the implications under international law. During the night, Shimon Peres had also sought the support of the former Defense Minister Moshe Dayan. Shortly after 0900hrs, the select ministerial team of Rabin, Peres, and Allon convened in the prime minister's office. One of the pressing considerations was whether Operation *Thunderbolt* would contravene U.S. government regulations that American military equipment could only be used for the purposes of legitimate self-defense. Any breach of these conditions entitled the United States to demand recovery of the equipment and cease all arms shipments to the offending country.

At 1100hrs a meeting of the inner circle of ministers who had been privy to the hostage crisis throughout the last week was convened. Prime Minister Yitzhak Rabin reviewed all the risks involved and stressed the implications of failure. There followed a further meeting of the full cabinet with all 19 ministers being summoned to the Kirya. Knowing he would not drive on the Sabbath, Yitzhak Rabin offered to send his official car to collect one minister, Zebulun Hammer, who was a strict Orthodox Jew. Hammer declined and decided to walk instead so as to maintain his religious observances. The trip took one and a half hours on foot. By the time he arrived the atmosphere at the Kirya was somber, with most ministers expecting the cabinet agenda to contain just one item—a decision to accede to the terrorists' demands before the looming deadline, just 24 hours away. Such gloomy predictions gave way to astonishment as Gen Motta Gur spread maps, sketches, and photographs across the table and began yet another detailed briefing. There might be an alternative to surrender, but the heavy risk of casualties weighed on everybody's minds and the debate continued long into the afternoon. Such a decision was too important to rush.

OPERATION *THUNDERBOLT*— KADUR HA-RA'AM

Rhinos to Africa

In the meantime, the first Hercules took off from Lod Airport at 1320hrs. As it was the Sabbath, the remaining four aircraft followed at five-minute intervals, each heading in a different direction; a fleet of aircraft flying in formation would have been too obvious to inquisitive eyes below on the beaches of Tel Aviv, Eilat, or Netanya, let alone to Soviet surveillance ships. At the very last moment, vital intelligence arrived. As Dan Shomron later recalled:

> When we were already on the plane before takeoff to Sharm el-Sheikh, there appeared a car with a driver with a case of documents in his hands, asking where is "Kaka" [the head of the Mossad, Yitzhak "Kaka" Hofi]. Kaka's in a government meeting in Jerusalem, we tell him and he starts to get back in the car. My intelligence officer, a most alert young man, Amnon Biran, jumps on him and really tears the package out of his hands. "That's not for you, it's for Kaka," the man shouts, and we tell him: "It's precisely for us." We climbed back up on the plane, opened the envelope and there were good photos of the area.

These were the aerial photographs of Entebbe Airport taken by the Mossad agent from his "stricken" plane just the day before, including crucial shots of the Old Terminal.

The Hercules flew nap-of-the-earth and in complete radio silence to avoid Soviet surveillance vessels in the Mediterranean Sea. Their efforts were almost compromised by a pilot of the Israeli airline Avira who, as the Karnafs came in to land at Ofira, broadcast to the world: "There seems to be a party going on down there." The

The Lockheed C-130 Hercules was critical to the success of Operation *Thunderbolt*. In the Israeli Air Force or Chel Ha'Avir, the C-130 Hercules is known as Karnaf or Rhinoceros. By July 1976, there were two squadrons of the C-130H model in service with No. 103 "Flying Elephant" and No. 131 "Yellow Bird." The latter undertook the raid on Entebbe. There were also two KC-130H aerial refueling aircraft within No. 103 Squadron at the time of Operation *Thunderbolt,* and it remains a mystery as to whether they actually took part in the mission.

Hercules aircraft congregated at Ofira, since it was the southernmost air base in the Sinai Peninsula. There they were topped up with fuel for the final 2,484-mile (3,998-km), eight-hour flight to Entebbe. "The flight to Sharm el-Sheikh was the most difficult I had ever had," recounts Amir Ofer, echoing the feelings of his comrades in arms. "I threw up many times, it was very hot. Flying beneath the radar there was so much turbulence. When I got to Sharm el-Sheikh, I couldn't take it anymore. The doctor gave me [air sickness] pills to take. And I was so afraid that I would collapse that I took one every hour for the rest of the flight." The aircraft were soon awash with vomit, and on arrival at Ofira, one soldier of the assault team was so ill that he could not continue and had to be replaced by Sgt Amos Goren. Once on the ground, the members of the Sayeret Matkal teams changed into Ugandan paratroopers' camouflage uniforms and green berets (items that had been manufactured in Israel when there had still been an IDF military mission in Uganda). As the ground force commander, Dan Shomron had to make a critical decision:

> When we reached Ofira there still wasn't an approval and so I arranged with "Froika" [BrigGen Ephraim Furer, the Military Secretary to the prime minister] that we would set out to Entebbe and that we had four to five hours' flight time to the point of no return, so that if the government did not approve the operation, we would be able to turn back. I admit that a decision like that would have saddened me very much. But after a few minutes "Froika" gave me the go-ahead for this arrangement and I understood from this that the prime minister was basically inclined towards approving the operation.

While at Ofira, Yoni Netanyahu gave his troops a final briefing. As always, he had a book tucked into his webbing. This one was a thriller novel by Alistair MacLean. Its title was *The Way to Dusty Death*.

With temperatures over 100 degrees Fahrenheit (37.8 degrees Celsius), the grossly overladen transport planes clawed their way skyward through the thin desert air after lumbering along the whole length of the undulating runway. They needed virtually every inch of its 1.5-mile (2.4-km) length. The normal takeoff weight was 155,000 pounds (70,307 kg). In wartime, permission was usually granted for a maximum weight of 175,000 pounds (79,379 kg) but on take off from Ofira Air Base, the load was a staggering 180,000 pounds (81,647 kg). The prevailing winds and weather required the aircraft to take off northward for at least 15 miles (24 km) before attempting to bank gently, no more than five degrees at a time, or else they would vibrate and shudder to the point of stalling. Due to the wideness of their turns, the aircraft were forced to encroach Saudi Arabian airspace before they could head on a southerly course. Having evaded this hazard, they then faced the gauntlet of the Red Sea with hostile nations to each side. Flying in loose formation, the aircraft maintained a height of less than 100 feet (30 m) to avoid radar detection, with the pilots periodically updating the pressure altimeter from the radar altimeter. The aircrew kept constant radar watch for ships below so that if necessary, the air armada could alter course to avoid being sighted. These maneuvers caused repeated deviations from the planned flight path. Each time it took careful calibration by the navigators to return to the correct course. Such flying was immensely tiring, and each pilot undertook little more than 15 minutes at the controls at a time. Once clear of the major Egyptian and Saudi Arabian radar sites, but before coming into range of the French surveillance facility in Djibouti and the Soviet one at Berbera in Somalia, the Hercules turned southward over Ethiopia. There they rose to a height of 2,000 feet (610 m), above

Lake
Victoria

Entebbe
22 miles (35 km)

Israeli
C-130 Hercules
transport

Old Terminal

Control
Tower

Military runway

New
Terminal

Air France
Airbus

Main runway

Lake Victoria

ENTEBBE AIRPORT

small arms range but below the capabilities of the rudimentary air traffic control system in the country.

Several hours after the Hercules had taken off, the two Boeing 707s took to the air from Lod Airport, their higher speed allowing them to arrive over Kenya at the same time as the transport aircraft. In their improvised colors, the converted airliners flew at a conventional height following the standard El Al route to the Republic of South Africa.

Back at the Kirya, the cabinet meeting continued to debate the possibility of heavy casualties with Prime Minister Yitzhak Rabin presenting an estimate of between 15 and 20 fatalities. Eventually, the cabinet gave its unanimous agreement for Operation *Thunderbolt* to proceed. Even so, Rabin then sought the approval of the Chairman of the Knesset Foreign Affairs and Security Committee, Itzhak Navon, and the Knesset opposition leaders, Menachem Begin and Elimelech Rimalt. Ordinarily Israeli politics are deeply divisive but all three gave their unreserved support, despite the estimate of casualties, to which the hardline Begin responded: "One must always hope for the best. One must believe and try to ensure that there will be no casualties. But if, Heaven forfend, these happen, they'll be of people who fell in battle and not as victims of butchery and savagery." He concluded with the words: "May The Almighty bless the way of the warriors."

"We've Come to Take You Home"

Accounts differ as to when Operation *Thunderbolt* was actually authorized; some members of The Unit believed it was at Ofira, while LtCol Joshua Shani has no recollection of ever receiving the order. As commander of the ground operation, BrigGen Dan Shomron was in the lead Karnaf with Shani and recalls: "Somewhere over Ethiopia we received a cryptic message—'Efrez. Mazel tov. Authorized. Good Luck.'" The aircraft continued to plough through the tropical night.

For Operation *Thunderbolt*, three of the four C-130 Hercules aircraft that landed at Entebbe had significantly greater payloads than permitted even in wartime. The four aircraft were 4X-FBA/102, 4X-FBB/106, 4X-FBQ/420, and 4X-FBT/435. Here, a 4X-FBB discharges various vehicles during an Israeli Air Force Day demonstration. Above the registration number is the insignia of No. 120 "International" Squadron that was first equipped with the C-130 in Israeli service in October 1971 operating out of Lod Airport.

In the Old Terminal at Entebbe, the plight of the hostages was now perilous. Many had already fallen ill with diarrhea and vomiting after eating contaminated meat. The coming of the Sabbath had been marked with the pitiful lighting of a couple of candles, and morale continued to decline as the deadline loomed. It had dropped even further following another visit by President Idi Amin at 1645hrs on his premature return from Mauritius, and the hostages had to face another uncomfortable night in the sultry heat. Only the young retained any optimism as they played their endless games of football with an old cola can. Benny Davidson, only 12 years old, even assured his mother that the IDF would come to rescue them that very night. His mother, Sarah Davidson, remained unconvinced as she was unable to conceive how the IDF could implement a rescue operation at such a vast distance.

Unknown to her, that distance was diminishing rapidly by the mile. The Hercules were thundering above the jungle canopy of Africa. With the remarkable facility some soldiers have when facing action, many slept in, on, or under the vehicles. Others found sleep impossible. Most were exhausted from the days of intensive training and rehearsal, and from the atrocious flight to Ofira. With 30 minutes remaining to touchdown, everyone was roused for a final equipment check. Rani Cohen, who had fallen asleep soon after leaving Ofira in the belief the mission would be canceled mid-flight, was extremely surprised to find he was now approaching Uganda. The assault teams took turns to focus the tactical lights on their Kalashnikovs at the optimum killing distance. Yoni Netanyahu moved among his men with words of encouragement and advice. Over northern Kenya, the air armada encountered a massive tropical storm. There was no way around it. As the aircraft pounded on, horribly buffeted, the dreadful, debilitating scourge of airsickness returned to many of the assault force. However, in some ways the storm worked to their advantage as it degraded the radar systems over East Africa. As streaks of lightning flashed through the night and thunderclaps cracked loudly above the noise of the engines, Operation *Thunderbolt* seemed to be a most appropriate name for such a mission. Above Kisuma, the aircraft wheeled right toward Lake Victoria, dipping low over the vast inland sea. Circling high above, the command and control Boeing carried generals Adam and Peled and their communications team. Shortly before 2300hrs, Kuti Adam sent the terse message to Tel Aviv: "Over Jordan!" denoting the air armada was in fact over Lake Victoria. The second Boeing 707 had already landed at Nairobi Airport at 2225hrs and, in the event that the Kenyan government would give permission for the rescue aircraft to land, the medical teams immediately prepared the operating theaters for the expected casualties. While three of the Hercules circled low above the lake, Shani turned toward Uganda. The AWADS radar picked up the airport at 2 miles (3 km) out, but no runway lights were discernible through the rain until, at the last moment, they became faintly visible. This was the critical moment. The Karnaf flared and landed. The length of the runway allowed it to slow down using only the brakes, not needing to use the reverse thrust, which would have created excessive noise. The inboard engines were immediately cut to reduce the sound signature further. Joshua Shani briefly clicked on his radio to relay the safe landing. Even as the C-130 was rolling to a halt, troops

---

4 Official IDF accounts of the raid state that the timing of the landing of the C-130 Hercules was to coincide with the departure of a British Airways flight so that the runway landing lights would still be illuminated. This has been reiterated in numerous books and accounts of the raid. However, British Airways records confirm that their only aircraft to land at Entebbe on July 3, 1976, arrived and left much earlier. Flight BA91 left London at 2000hrs on Friday July 2 and landed at Entebbe at 0555hrs on July 3 before flying on to Nairobi in Kenya arriving at 0745hrs. On its return trip, Flight BA90 departed Nairobi at 1015hrs but flew to London via Addis Ababa and not Entebbe.

OPERATION *THUNDERBOLT*: THE INITIAL ASSAULT
July 3, 1976

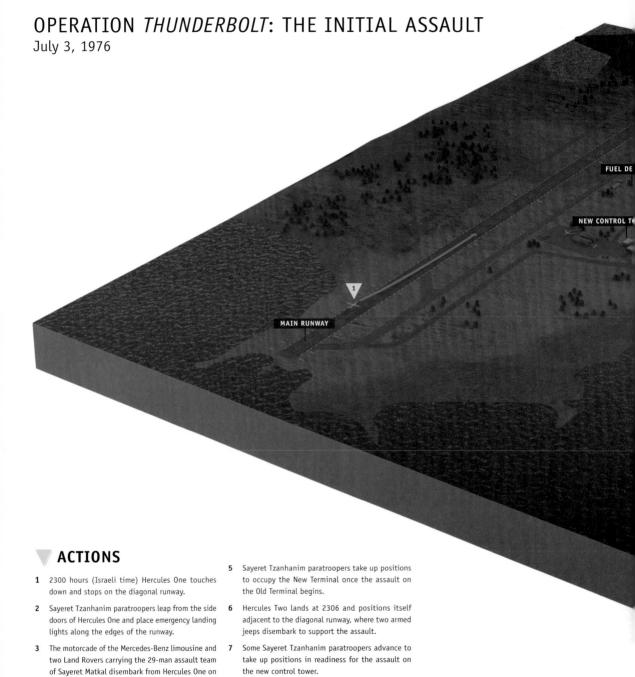

FUEL DE

NEW CONTROL T

1

MAIN RUNWAY

▼ ACTIONS

1   2300 hours (Israeli time) Hercules One touches down and stops on the diagonal runway.

2   Sayeret Tzanhanim paratroopers leap from the side doors of Hercules One and place emergency landing lights along the edges of the runway.

3   The motorcade of the Mercedes-Benz limousine and two Land Rovers carrying the 29-man assault team of Sayeret Matkal disembark from Hercules One on the diagonal runway and drives toward the Old Terminal at a steady speed.

4   Sayeret Tzanhanim paratroopers then advance toward the New Terminal building.

5   Sayeret Tzanhanim paratroopers take up positions to occupy the New Terminal once the assault on the Old Terminal begins.

6   Hercules Two lands at 2306 and positions itself adjacent to the diagonal runway, where two armed jeeps disembark to support the assault.

7   Some Sayeret Tzanhanim paratroopers advance to take up positions in readiness for the assault on the new control tower.

8   With Hercules Three just 200 feet (61 m) above the ground, the airport lights are switched off, but fortunately the emergency lights placed by the paratroopers allow it to land safely.

2

4

3

NEW TERMINAL

OLD TERMINAL

AIR FRANCE AIRBUS

MILITARY RUNWAY

LAKE VICTORIA

HERCULES ONE

HERCULES TWO

6

HERCULES THREE

NEW TERMINAL

FUEL DEPOT

8

7

NEW CONTROL TOWER

of Sayeret Tzanhanim jumped out to place emergency landing lights for the following aircraft.[4]

Prior to landing, Amitzur Kafri said a prayer as he turned the ignition of the Mercedes-Benz. It fired the first time. In the back of the second Land Rover, Amir Ofer began to prepare for the impending assault on the Old Terminal building:

> The moment that the wheels touched the ground I immediately loaded my weapon— a Klatch [AK47 Kalashnikov]. One of my friends shouted: "Don't load your weapon in the plane." But I told him to shut up. This is a real war. No rules anymore! Then when the rear ramp opened I was expecting to see tigers or lions or giraffes or whatever on the airfield but there was nothing, it was a standard airstrip like everywhere else in the world.

The lead Karnaf turned on to the taxiway to the Old Terminal and stopped. It was just 30 seconds behind schedule, 2300hrs Israeli time, midnight in Uganda. The rear ramp was lowered fully and the three vehicles disembarked. Muki Betser broke radio silence for a moment and sent the codeword to the assault teams for all weapons to be set to single-shot mode for selective firing so as to minimize danger to the hostages. At a steady 25 miles per hour (40 km per hour), they motored in procession toward the Old Terminal, its bright lights spilling out onto the rain-slicked concrete. Some 275 yards (251 m) short, a Ugandan soldier appeared on each side of the approach road. The one to the right raised his rifle at the approaching vehicles. The other disappeared into the darkness. Sitting in the front passenger seat closest to the threat, Yoni Netanyahu made an instant decision. He barked an order to the driver to cut to the right enabling a clear line of fire as behind him, and Giora Zusman cocked his .22cal Beretta pistol fitted with a silencer. Both Netanyahu and Zusman fired repeatedly at a distance of some 33 feet (10 m). The Ugandan soldier fell to the ground, but the small caliber rounds were not sufficient to kill him. As he staggered to his feet and aimed his rifle at the Mercedes-Benz, the sharp crack of a Kalashnikov was heard from the following Land Rover, shattering the stillness of the night. Immediately the other Ugandan soldier reappeared on the roadway, illuminated by the headlights of the car. Sgt Amnon Peled, manning the vehicle-mounted machine gun of the following Land Rover, fired a burst but missed. Clamping his GPMG tighter, he fired another long burst as the Ugandan ran into the stream of bullets.

All secrecy was now lost in the fusillade of gunfire. Yoni Netanyahu ordered Kafri to drive as fast as possible to the Old Terminal, but now the Ugandan guards began to open fire, with those on the control tower having a clear view of the approaching vehicles. Realizing immediately how vulnerable his Sayeret Matkal fighters were in their packed vehicles, Netanyahu commanded the driver to get as close to the control tower as possible in order to reduce the angle of fire. Once there, he ordered Amitzur Kafri to stop. The men of The Unit leapt from the vehicles in some disorder as Netanyahu shouted to them to storm the building. The assault force was some 55 yards (50 m) short of it. To Muki Betser, the plan was unraveling before his eyes: "The tragedy of *Ma'alot* came back to me and the word *Ma'alot, Ma'alot* beat inside my head. I felt it was going to happen again." On the second floor of the Old Terminal, Capt Isaac Bakka of the Ugandan Air Force recalls: "I heard a plane landing and then I hear boots thumping. Some of the infantrymen who had been deployed around the terminal began to speak to each other in Swahili—'Maybe the Children of God are coming.' That was a joke among the soldiers who use the term for Israeli soldiers or Israeli people as the Children of God are described in the Bible." For many of them and for the terrorists, the joke was to be short-lived.

The Israeli troops charged forward with the assault teams becoming hopelessly intermingled. At the forefront, Muki Betser fired at the fleeting targets of Ugandan soldiers as they emerged out of the darkness. Spotting a terrorist outside the front doors of the Old Terminal, he again took aim, but his shots went wide and the terrorist ran back into the hostage area. He recalls:

> I knew I had used up most of the magazine creating the cover fire in order to reach the control tower. But I also knew that once inside I only needed a few bullets to do the job. Now, surprised by the terrorist, I aimed and fired. Only a couple of bullets spat out of the barrel and I missed. He ducked back into the building.

The terrorist was, in fact, Wilfred Böse, who burst back into the departure hall and aimed his weapon at the cowering hostages while reportedly shouting: "The Ugandans have gone crazy. They're shooting at us." Outside, Muki Betser hesitated by the corner of the building as he exchanged magazines on his weapon. Other soldiers followed suit. The assault momentarily faltered. The slightest delay could prove fatal for the hostages. Immediately, Yoni Netanyahu urged his troops onward as he rushed to the fore. Sprinting from the second Land Rover, Sgt Amir Ofer feared he was lagging behind his team leader, Lt Amnon Peled, but he was the first to reach the hall containing the hostages. Ofer vividly recalls the moment as he ran to the entrance door and came face to face with a gunman:

> The glass was broken by someone lying on the floor shooting automatic gunfire at me— the bullets flashed one to the right, one to the left, one beneath my legs, one behind my legs, one past my left ear… I counted later what was left in his magazine, he had shot about 15 bullets at me, only God knows how he missed me, there was not even a mark on me—it was amazing. The range was something like (23–33 ft.) [7–10 m]… We shot at each other and finally I saw his head drop. I rushed in, shot him again, looked to the right and realized I was unintentionally alone. I was the first to arrive.

Fayez Abdul-Rahim Jaber was the first terrorist to die.

Unknown to Ofer, Wilfred Böse and Brigitte Kuhlmann were crouching on the ground to his left. They immediately turned their guns in his direction as if to shoot him in the back. At that moment Amnon Peled burst through the doors killing them both in a barrage of automatic gunfire. Tragically, the random fire from Fayez Jaber prior to his death had found its mark. Outside, Yoni Netanyahu slumped to the ground with gunshot wounds to the chest and arm. The Unit doctor David Hassin, along with members of the command group, dragged Netanyahu's bleeding body to the limited cover of an open lattice wall that ran parallel to the terminal building. There, Hassin began emergency treatment but within moments he realized that Yoni Netanyahu was severely wounded.

Mindful of Netanyahu's specific orders not to stop for the fallen, his soldiers continued the assault. Amos Goren and Muki Betser charged into the main hall as a second Palestinian terrorist emerged from behind a concrete column and raised his Kalashnikov. In a remarkable stroke of good fortune, Goren's bullet struck the cylinder of the terrorist's gun, preventing the ejection of ammunition despite the fact that it had already been fired.

Two hostages, 56-year-old Ida Borochovitch, a Russian Jew who had emigrated to Israel, and 52-year-old Pasco Cohen, a medical insurance fund manager, were fatally

OVERLEAF
At the moment of the Sayeret Matkal assault, Sgt Amir Ofer returns fire through the glass doors of the Old Terminal building, killing the terrorist Fayez Abdul-Rahim Jaber. Attached to his webbing is a bullhorn to give instructions to the hostages while on his back is a knapsack containing demolition charges. Behind him are Amos Goren and Muki Betser, who was in command of the assault force. Rushing past them is the assault team commanded by Danny Arditi, whose task was to eliminate the terrorists in their living quarters at the end of the Old Terminal. In the middle ground, another assault team is attacking the Old Terminal. To their rear is the command team of LtCol Yoni Netanyahu shown at the moment when he was hit and mortally wounded by terrorist fire from within the Old Terminal. In the background is the assault team of Capt Yiftah Reicher as they attack the Customs Hall and second floor of the Old Terminal, where most of the Ugandan soldiers were billeted. Stationed close to the Mercedes-Benz limousine and the two Land Rovers in the far background, the Arnon Epstein's support team is attempting to suppress the fire from the old Control Tower that was to delay the evacuation of the hostages until it had been fully eliminated.

injured in the crossfire. Borochovitch had been shot in the heart and Cohen in the pelvis. Hostage Ilan Hartuv, the son of Dora Bloch, recalls the moment the gunfire erupted:

> We heard shooting and saw what looked like tracer fire. We realized somebody was shooting at the terrorists but we didn't know who it was. Then the soldiers started pouring in and although they were dressed like Ugandans I said it was the *Tzahal* [Israeli Army] and everybody started shouting: "*Nes! Nes!*" [Hebrew for miracle]. When the Israelis arrived we couldn't believe it. We had talked a lot about the possibility and we even had two reserve colonels from the Israeli Air Force among us who said it couldn't be done.

As the gunfire subsided, a dark figure jumped up from the floor. He was immediately cut down by automatic fire. Tragically, it was a 19-year-old French Jew named Jean-Jacques Maimoni. A survivor of the Nazi concentration camps, Yitzhak David, went to his aid but was shot through the left shoulder and the bullet entered his lung. Remembering the megaphones they were carrying, both Amir Ofer and Amos Goren barked out orders in English and Hebrew: "*Koolam lishkav!* Everybody lie down! *Tzahal!* We are the Israeli Army!" Despite these instructions, another shape rose up from the ground. Two Kalashnikovs were immediately trained on the figure but in the split second before firing, Peled and Goren realized it was a little girl and raised their rifles. An older man also stood up, but the other hostages shouted at the soldiers to hold their fire. Like many captives, Sarah Davidson had whiled away the weary hours in the oppressive heat playing endless games of cards. She later recounted the moment when the hostages realized that their rescue was at hand:

> Suddenly we hear a shot followed by a burst. We throw the cards down and exchange looks. The terrorists reach for their weapons. They seemed confused. In a split second we dive to the ground…The shooting subsides. Someone shouts "Israeli soldiers." Are we saved? We lift our heads slowly in disbelief and we see the most magnificent sight of our lives—like a dream, a short soldier, his face darkened, in battle fatigues wearing a white hat and holding a large machine gun. He looks at us calmly and says: "Are you all right? Come on we've come to take you home."

All four terrorists guarding the hostages were dead. The shooting had lasted little more than 45 seconds. No doubt it was with relief that Muki Betser radioed to the command group: "Have hostages. Team intact. No casualties." The response he received was as ominous as it was brief: "Yoni's down!"

99 Minutes at Entebbe

Just four minutes had passed from the moment the first Hercules touched down until the four terrorists guarding the hostages had been killed. The carefully planned element of surprise had succeeded but at the cost of four dead or dying Israelis, one for each terrorist eliminated in the departure hall.

Meanwhile, the other assault forces were attacking their designated targets. The team under the command of Lt Amos Ben-Avraham stormed into the main hall as the firing subsided. Soldiers from various assault teams raced for the end doors of the building where the terrorists had made their living quarters. The "Room of Separation" was also situated in this area, but Israeli intelligence did not know whether any hostages were still being held there. Lt Giora Zusman was the first to enter. He sprayed the room with automatic fire, noting the pile of Israeli passports on the table. As there was no one to cover him, he retired outside to the hallway to reload. Just then, two members of his team raced past, firing into the kitchen area at the end of the hallway. They found two dead Ugandan soldiers slumped on the floor. Shlomo Reisman and Ilan Blumer soon arrived, although they had both been assigned to Amnon Peled's team. Men of yet another team commanded by Danny Arditi were trying to enter the terrorists' living quarters via another door, but it was locked. One of his men threw a hand grenade through the window but on hitting the frame, it bounced back. In the ensuing explosion, one soldier was wounded in the leg by shrapnel.

Zusman and Reisman ventured farther into the smoke-filled building followed by Tamir Prado, Yoni's radioman. They soon encountered two men dressed in civilian clothes with no obvious weapons and their hands raised distractedly. Zusman passed them by thinking they were hostages, but Reisman noticed a webbing belt with grenades attached. Unable to fire since Zusman was in his line of attack, he shouted: "They're terrorists! Shoot them!" but Zusman called back: "No. They're hostages!" Stepping aside to get a clear angle, Reisman shot them dead. A primed grenade rolled from a lifeless hand. The Israelis threw themselves to the ground. Fortunately, the bodies of the dead terrorists absorbed the force of the blast along with most of the grenade fragments, and Reisman only suffered a cut lip. By now Danny Arditi's team had penetrated the building and was engaged in clearing the remaining rooms, assisted by Amos Ben-Avraham and his squad. Once the area was secured, the body of another terrorist was found. The final terrorist death toll amounted to seven, comprising the two Germans Wilfred Böse and Brigitte Kuhlmann, and five Palestinians—Fayez Abdul-Rahim Jaber, Abu Ali, Abdul Razag, Khaled al-Khalil, and Jayel Naji al-Arjam. All were fingerprinted and photographed for positive identification later. The other three terrorists including the leader, Fouad Awad, were staying the night in Kampala and thus escaped with their lives.

At the other end of the building, the team of Capt Yiftah Reicher attacked the customs hall and the second floor of the Old Terminal, where the Ugandan soldiers were quartered. The ground floor was quickly cleared with several Ugandan military killed. Two more were shot dead at the top of the stairs. Leaving one member of the team to cover the corridor, doorways, and staircase, Reicher and Rani Cohen rushed into the end room. This had once been a restaurant but was now the sleeping area for the Ugandan soldiers. Festooned with blankets and sleeping bags, it was deserted. Most of the soldiers had fled from the "Children of God" at the outset of the assault, jumping out of the second floor windows and fleeing into the night. As they turned to go back, Reicher and Cohen both saw the silhouette of two figures. They opened fire simultaneously. A shattering of glass revealed that they had shot at themselves in a mirror. They then climbed up on to the roof of the building that had once been a canopied drinking and dining area. From there they witnessed the ongoing firefight between the support team of Arnon Epstein together with the soldiers manning the machine guns on the Land Rovers, and the Ugandan soldiers firing down from the control tower. As planned, Epstein's team had followed Reicher and his men into the customs hall but, after killing some of the African soldiers missed by the first assault team, they were unable to find the stairs. As the tempo of firing increased outside, they returned to the aircraft apron to engage the Ugandan troops in the control tower. The latter's stubborn resistance was to continue for some time.

Throughout the assault at the Old Terminal, BrigGen Dan Shomron had waited near the end of the runway with his senior communications officer, LtCol Haim Oren, and three other officers of his command group. Until the arrival of the second

OPERATION *THUNDERBOLT*: THE ASSAULT AND THE EVACUATION
July 3, 1976

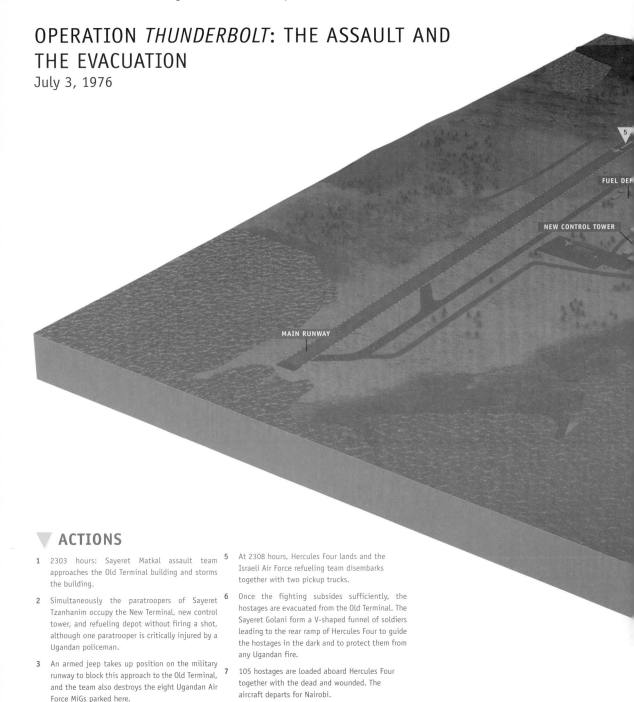

FUEL DE[POT]

NEW CONTROL TOWER

MAIN RUNWAY

▼ ACTIONS

1   2303 hours: Sayeret Matkal assault team approaches the Old Terminal building and storms the building.

2   Simultaneously the paratroopers of Sayeret Tzanhanim occupy the New Terminal, new control tower, and refueling depot without firing a shot, although one paratrooper is critically injured by a Ugandan policeman.

3   An armed jeep takes up position on the military runway to block this approach to the Old Terminal, and the team also destroys the eight Ugandan Air Force MiGs parked here.

4   While one armed jeep engages the Old Control Tower, the other two jeeps cover the area to the immediate north of the Old Terminal.

5   At 2308 hours, Hercules Four lands and the Israeli Air Force refueling team disembarks together with two pickup trucks.

6   Once the fighting subsides sufficiently, the hostages are evacuated from the Old Terminal. The Sayeret Golani form a V-shaped funnel of soldiers leading to the rear ramp of Hercules Four to guide the hostages in the dark and to protect them from any Ugandan fire.

7   105 hostages are loaded aboard Hercules Four together with the dead and wounded. The aircraft departs for Nairobi.

8   0040 hours: Hercules Two and Three depart from Entebbe with all the remaining troops and vehicles.

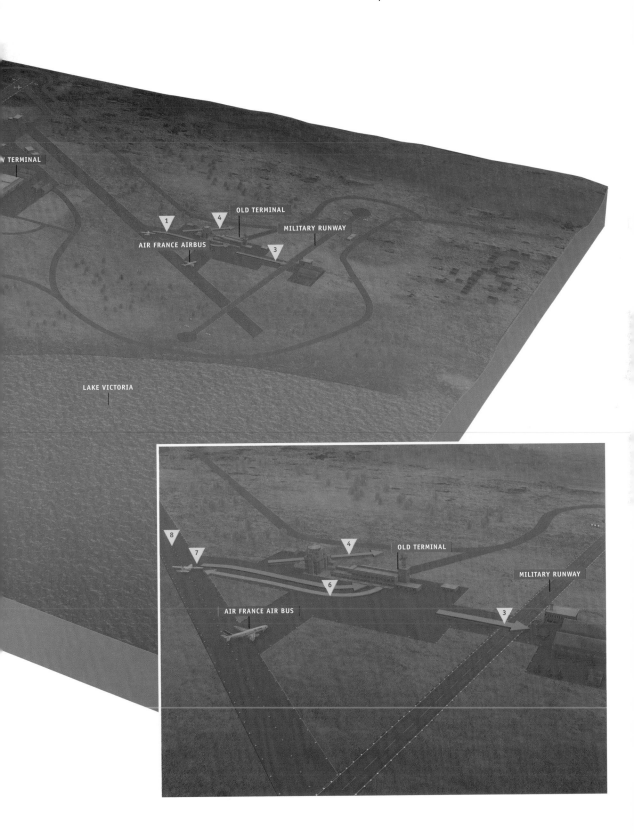

W TERMINAL

OLD TERMINAL

1

4

AIR FRANCE AIRBUS

MILITARY RUNWAY

3

LAKE VICTORIA

8

7

4

OLD TERMINAL

6

MILITARY RUNWAY

AIR FRANCE AIR BUS

3

Hercules with his communications vehicle, there was little he could do but watch his paratroops attack the New Terminal once firing by the Sayeret Matkal had commenced. Exactly on schedule the second Hercules, piloted by LtCol Nathan "Nati" Dvir, came in to land six minutes after the first. As it taxied along the runway, an airport fire truck with flashing lights drove along the adjoining service road. Suddenly it stopped and its lights went out. Moments later, in three distinct phases, the main runway lights, the lights along the taxiways, and then those illuminating the aircraft apron were also extinguished. Nevertheless the two armed jeeps under the command of Maj Shaul Mofaz, as well as Shomron's command vehicle, were swiftly unloaded. LtCol Amnon Biran, Intelligence Officer of the Infantry and Paratroop Command, immediately erected the radio antenna to establish communications with the forces on the ground and the airborne command aircraft. Driven by LtCol Moshe Shapiro, the jeep promptly picked up Shomron and the remainder of his command group and followed the armed jeeps to the Old Terminal. Meanwhile, as the runway was plunged into darkness, the third Hercules carrying the other two armed jeeps was coming in to land. With the plane just 300 feet (41 m) above the landing strip, the pilot showed commendable skill, slowing his descent until the aircraft was squarely aligned with the emergency beacons before putting the heavily laden Karnaf down on the second half of the runway. With no noise constraints, Arieh Oz immediately engaged full reverse thrust and braked hard to bring the Hercules to a shuddering halt. The second pair of armed jeeps were hastily unloaded and driven to the Old Terminal in support of the other two vehicles. The fourth C-130 Hercules landed soon afterward and by 2308hrs, all four aircraft were on the ground.

As soon as the firefight began at the Old Terminal, the paratroopers of the Sayeret Tzanhanim rushed forward to storm the New Terminal, the control tower, and the associated airport facilities, including the fuel storage compound. Under the command of Col Matan Vilnai, the buildings were quickly captured. Few people were inside except some civilians, airport workers, and policemen who were corralled together without a shot being fired. In order to prevent any bullets from being accidentally discharged among the civilians, the paratroopers were ordered to keep the safety catches engaged on their Galil rifles. However, during a search of the upper floors tragedy struck. Sgt Surin Hershko, just days away from completing his military service, was climbing a stairwell with a central column that obscured upward vision.

Prime Minister Benjamin Netanyahu proposes a toast with Gen Shaul Mofaz who was the 16th IDF Chief of Staff between 1996 and 1999. The red beret identifies Gen Mofaz as a paratrooper, but during the raid on Entebbe he was a member of Sayeret Matkal when he commanded the contingent of Armored Fighting Vehicles that acted as a protection force against intervention by the Ugandan Army. As the younger brother of Yoni, Benjamin Netanyahu stated: "Yonatan's death at Entebbe marked a unique turning point in the world's battle against terrorism. After Entebbe, it was very difficult to argue that you had no choice but to surrender to terrorism." Following the Entebbe raid, Netanyahu founded the Yonatan Institute for the Study of Terrorism.

Suddenly he encountered a Ugandan civilian and policeman coming down toward him. The policeman had a pistol in his hand and immediately fired two shots at a range of 3 feet (.9 m). The first missed, but the second struck Hershko in the neck. He fell to the floor bleeding profusely. These were the only shots fired during the whole operation to occupy the New Terminal. The bullet lodged in Hershko's spine and he was paralyzed for life as a quadriplegic. Once the control tower was occupied, the Israeli Air Force technicians ascertained where the master switches were located to operate the runway lights in order to allow the Hercules to take off again. They also established a refueling capability for the aircraft with the portable pump they had brought with them as a backup.

By now, Dan Shomron had learned that Yoni Netanyahu had been wounded and Muki Betser had assumed command of the Sayeret Matkal contingent. The stubborn resistance from the Ugandan troops on the control tower precluded the immediate evacuation of the hostages, even though the fourth Hercules had landed and was now waiting for the order to approach the Old Terminal. Under the direction of Arik Ron from Netanyahu's command group, Maj Shaul Mofaz brought the firepower of his armed jeep to bear on the control tower, causing its .50cal machine guns and RPGs to gouge large chunks out of the structure. As planned, the companion jeep took up position covering the military runway and its MiG jets, while the second pair of jeeps covered the approach roads from Kampala to the north of the Old Terminal. Meanwhile, Yoni Netanyahu was evacuated on one of the Land Rovers to Dr. Ephraim Sneh's medical staff who had landed in the last Hercules. There, Dr. Eran Dolev and the resuscitation team fought desperately to save his life, but he had suffered almost total blood loss and, despite their best efforts, his life ebbed away.

When the firing at the control tower had subsided sufficiently, the fourth Karnaf with its 16-man contingent of Sayeret Golani was called forward. Once in position some 165 yards (151 m) from the Old Terminal, the Golani soldiers formed a funnel toward the rear ramp of the aircraft to prevent distracted hostages from wandering off into the dark. Chaos reigned inside the main hall as the former captives rummaged around for their belongings, despite being ordered to leave immediately; one, incredibly, insisted on returning to collect his duty-free goods. Precious minutes were lost as some insisted on dragging their luggage with them, overcrowding the Land Rovers as they were shuttled to the waiting C-130. When the hostages emerged, renewed firing erupted from the control tower. Once more, the jeep poured fire into the building until the fusillade diminished. Inside the hall, there was pandemonium. Some hostages were still seeking treasured items or even their shoes. Clad only in her underwear because of the heat, one of the female Air France flight attendants went into panic after suffering slight wounds from ricochet rounds. Amir Ofer was ordered to carry her to the waiting vehicles at the precise moment that the firing outside resumed. As Amir Ofer later recounted: "I threw her over my shoulder and went outside. Suddenly a bullet flew by my head…"

The Peugeot pickup arrived to transport the dead and seriously injured to the aircraft, where they were placed in litters in the forward cargo hold behind the cockpit. Slowly, the hostages crowded into the fuselage. The head of each family was required to account for all his kin and even Capt Michel Bacos had to report whether all members of his Air France crew were present. Even so the numbers did not tally. One hostage was definitely missing. The day before, 75-year-old Dora Bloch had choked on a piece of meat and had been taken to Mulago Hospital in Kampala. Her son, Ilan Hartuv, approached Dr. Eran Dolev to see whether he should stay behind but was told that if he did so, he would undoubtedly put his life at risk and that the only real option was for him to leave with the other hostages. The pilot of the Karnaf,

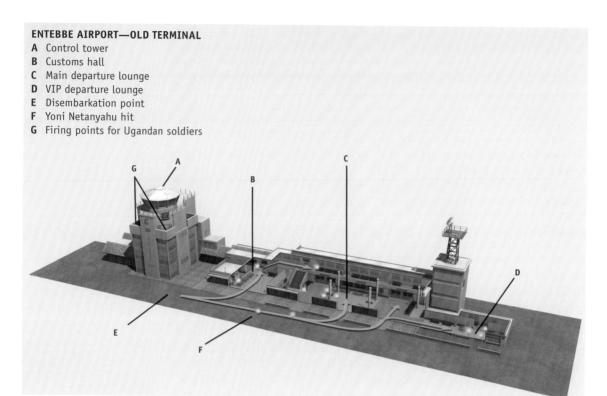

ENTEBBE AIRPORT—OLD TERMINAL
A Control tower
B Customs hall
C Main departure lounge
D VIP departure lounge
E Disembarkation point
F Yoni Netanyahu hit
G Firing points for Ugandan soldiers

JULY 03, 1976

1320–1340hrs: Hercules aircraft take off from Lod Airport.

JULY 03, 1976

2300hrs: Assault team lands at Entebbe Airport.

LtCol Amnon Halivni, insisted that the loadmaster present a written manifest of the hostages to ensure that no one was left behind. Again the number came to 93, plus the bodies of the two hostages killed. After repeated counts, the numbers still did not agree, but the hostages themselves insisted that everyone was accounted for except the unfortunate Dora Bloch. Indeed there were 105 hostages on board and the miscount was more than likely due to the overcrowding and chaotic situation on board. Amnon Halivni left his pilot's seat for the first time since Ofira to check for himself, but because of the mass of people, he was unable to get very far. Despite the roar of the engines, he noticed an uneasy silence inside the fuselage. He also identified Michel Bacos from his white shirt and pilot's insignia and invited him up onto the flight deck. The aircraft had been on the ground for 26 minutes near the Old Terminal. From his cockpit, Amnon Halivni could still see bursts of gunfire as the fighting at the control tower continued. He was only too aware of the vulnerability of his aircraft and its packed fuselage of hostages:

> We're sitting there with the engines running and tracers are flying in all directions. And what's a plane after all? It's a mass of tubes and wires and cables and anything can happen to it. And this one thought went through my head—God help Israel. Let the plane go without being hit.

At last, Halivni was given permission to take off. The Karnaf rolled down the taxiway to the main runway, where it immediately began to pick up speed past the three other C-130s waiting to refuel. The hostage aircraft lifted off at 1152hrs (1252hrs local time), just 51 minutes after the first Karnaf had landed. The aircraft climbed sharply over Lake Victoria and turned toward Kenya. After a week of fear and dread, the hostages were bound for freedom. Aluminium thermal blankets were distributed to ward off the cold in flight and were also used to shroud the dead. The C-130 had sufficient fuel for 90 minutes' flight time. To the crews of the other aircraft, it was a moment of great relief. The main objective of the raid, to secure the release of the overwhelming majority of the hostages, had been achieved.

Throughout the evacuation, the four armed jeeps had acted as a blocking force against Ugandan reinforcements from Kampala and had been used to subdue the troops at the airport. The stubborn resistance from the control tower required the unit commander, Maj Shaul Mofaz, to remain close by in his jeep and engage the position with direct fire. Time and again the fusillade from the tower was silenced, yet one particular Ugandan soldier would repeatedly return to the fray and continue the skirmish. One of the companion armed jeeps moved eastward to cover the military runway and its associated hangars and barracks. Five MiG-21 fighters were identified to the south of the runway and another three MiG-17s to the north. The vehicle commander, Omer Bar-Lev, sought permission to destroy them for, should their pilots return, they could well constitute a threat to the Hercules once they left Entebbe. The request was passed to Dan Shomron and to the airborne command post, but no answer was forthcoming. Eventually, the jeep crew took it upon themselves to destroy the fighters with heavy machine-gun fire. Several burst into flames illuminating the night sky, a useful act in itself as one of the other jeeps to the north of the Old Terminal had shot up the generator supplying electricity to the building. The burning aircraft provided sufficient light to complete a final search of the area, including the hijacked Airbus, for any stragglers. All that remained in the darkened departure hall were discarded clothes and eating utensils, jumbled mattresses and blankets, as well as the bullet-ridden bodies of the terrorists. To the north, Ugandan troops were observed approaching the airport but the leading truck halted several hundred yards short, flashing its headlights. The convoy gingerly approached, but at a range of 200 yards (183 m), the Israelis opened fire and the Ugandan column was stopped in its tracks.

As the last elements of the Sayeret Matkal assault teams withdrew in the Mercedes-Benz and the two Land Rovers, the lone Ugandan machine-gunner on the control tower opened fire again. Fortunately, as had happened throughout the firefight, his aim was poor and his shots went wide. In the Mercedes-Benz, Muki Betser expostulated: "God he's stubborn!" but out of a grudging respect for his sheer persistence, the Israelis did not return fire. Idi Amin subsequently decorated the soldier for bravery. As the rearguard, the jeeps remained on station patrolling the perimeter of the airport and guarding the road from Kampala, while the painfully slow process of refueling the aircraft continued. The aircraft crews waited anxiously for their charges and for information on the progress of the raid now that the hostages were flying to safety. However, the prolonged firefight at the control tower was over. The Sayeret Matkal team and their vehicles were loaded aboard Hercules One in reverse embarkation order to their arrival, with the Mercedes-Benz being first onto the aircraft. Then word came down the command chain that the Kenyan government had given permission for all the aircraft to be refueled at Jomo Kenyatta Airport in Nairobi. At 0012hrs (now Sunday July 4), Hercules One with the Sayeret Matkal contingent took off, bound for Nairobi. The jeeps now began a gradual withdrawal to the New Terminal, each leapfrogging the other so that the area to the north was continually dominated by their firepower. As they withdrew, the crews threw delayed action demolition blocks out of their vehicles along the runway to deter followers. Then, as they closed with the aircraft, smoke grenades were detonated to cover the vulnerable process of loading. Hercules Three, piloted by Arieh Oz, was loaded next and stood waiting on the main runway with its engines pounding. Finally, the last pair of jeeps under the command of Shaul Mofaz arrived

JULY 03, 1976

2352–0040 hrs: Hostages evacuated from Entebbe. Israeli troops take off from Entebbe Airport.

and quickly drove up the rear ramp of Hercules Two, followed by Dan Shomron's command jeep. Its pilot, Nati Dvir, had instructed Arieh Oz to await departure in case either C-130 was damaged and it became necessary to load all personnel onto just one aircraft. Threading their way through the gleam of the portable landing lights, the two laden Karnafs took to the air with Hercules Two lifting off at 0040hrs, one hour, and 39 minutes after the first C-130 had landed at Entebbe Airport.

Return to Israel

By now, Hercules Four, carrying the hostages and wounded, was nearing Nairobi Airport. During the flight, both Dr. Ephraim Sneh and Dr. Eran Dolev tried everything in their power to revive Yoni Netanyahu, but it was to no avail. The condition of each of the two seriously wounded hostages, Pasco Cohen and Yitzhak David, was stabilized and the lightly injured were treated for their wounds. The plane was heavy with emotion and studied silence. Dr. Jossi Faktor recalls:

> While there was jubilation, the passengers also appeared in a state of shock. This was expected. They had been captive for a week and then unexpectedly rescued in a shoot-out where they could so easily have lost their lives. Three of the hostages did. Compounding their trauma had been the constant fear of execution if their captors' demands were not met. So while there was the obvious feeling of elation, it was also mixed with sorrow at the loss of life.

Yet there could have been a much greater loss of life. Dr. Ephraim Sneh remembers being accosted by a lady with the words: "Major! Major! I'm afraid I'm sitting on some military thing." (He was in fact a colonel.) "She takes from under her... a mini-hand grenade." Sneh later went on to recount with humor and no small measure of relief:

> This was the sort of grenade [white phosphorous] notorious for its low safety, used only by Special Forces units for special operations. I think it fell from Yoni's gear when he was rushed aboard. The wounded were loaded before the hostages—so I believe that 100 or so hostages trod on this grenade. You can imagine what could have happened if that grenade had exploded in the Hercules holding all those hostages.

One by one the Hercules landed at Nairobi Airport followed by the airborne command post Boeing 707. Joshua Shani shut down the engines of his Karnaf for the first time since leaving Ofira some ten hours before.

The seriously wounded hostages were transferred to a hospital in Nairobi for emergency treatment, but tragically Pasco Cohen never recovered after surgery. Sgt Surin Hershko was placed aboard the Boeing 707 hospital aircraft, with a number of women and children from the main body of hostages, in order to fly back to Israel as quickly as possible. It was at Nairobi that the soldiers on the other planes were told of Yoni Netanyahu's death. Since he was responsible for weapons and ordnance, Amitzur Kafri recalls: "I went to see Yoni. It was very painful and I took his [combat] vest. It had two mini-grenades in it and a bullet had hit the top of his grenades and made a hole in his magazine. I saw it was lucky that it didn't explode in the plane or when he got hurt." With the Israeli aircraft ringed by armed Kenyan soldiers and members of the GSU, Gen Kuti Adam ordered each plane to depart as soon as it was refueled. The Hercules carrying most of the hostages and the dead was the first to take off at 0204hrs. The others followed in due course. All flew eastward out to the Indian

Ocean and then northward, around the Horn of Africa, through the Gulf of Aden and the Strait of Bab el Mandeb, and up the Red Sea to Israel and freedom. By this route, none of the aircraft crossed the territory of any potentially hostile country. With the last planes in the air, the personnel in the Chief of Staff's office allowed themselves a moment to celebrate with a few bottles of champagne, for they had not received a report of any deaths at this time. Old political foes Yitzhak Rabin and Menachem Begin hugged each other and shared a drink with a *L'Chaim* (Hebrew toast meaning "to life"). A spokesman for the Defense Ministry made a telephone call to Professor Gross, representing the relatives of the hostages, informing him of the outcome of the raid. Throughout the night, telephone lines across Israel were busy as family after family were given the news. Among them was a thrilled Robert Maimoni, the father of Jean-Jacques. At 0400hrs he roused his sleeping family in their apartment in the coastal town of Netanya, to announce that the IDF had freed the hostages in Entebbe. His wife, Rachel, and their daughter, Martine, were ecstatic at the news.

Triumph and Tragedy

The long 11-hour flight was uneventful until, with still over six hours' flying time to Israel, a Karnaf pilot tuned into the Israel Army Network radio station hoping to enjoy some music. The troops were outraged to hear an announcement about the raid on Entebbe, fearing that the operation might be compromised even at this late stage. Currently in airspace between Saudi Arabia and Egypt, it was possible that either country could send up fighter planes to intercept the lumbering transport aircraft. However, an alert reporter from the Agence France Presse had filed a wire story after learning of shots being fired at Entebbe Airport. The raid was now headline news in Paris and on the BBC in London. The troops in Hercules One were somewhat mollified when the pilot, hearing Idi Amin on shortwave radio, attached it to the loudspeaker so that all on board could hear the Ugandan President grandly announce that the airport had been reoccupied. Eventually, Israeli Air Force F-4 Phantom fighters arrived to escort the air armada home. As the aircraft flew low over the port of Eilat, the aircrews were astonished to see the streets and beaches packed with waving and cheering crowds. Hercules Four, with the hostages aboard, landed at Tel Nof Air Force Base at 0943hrs. The hostages were taken aside for a briefing and instructed not to reveal any operational details about the raid. One by one, the other aircraft landed. As the Sayeret Matkal soldiers trooped out of Hercules One, they were met by Prime Minister Yitzhak Rabin and Defense Minister Shimon Peres. The latter called to Muki Betser to ask how Yoni Netanyahu had been killed. His reply was succinct: "He went first. He fell first."

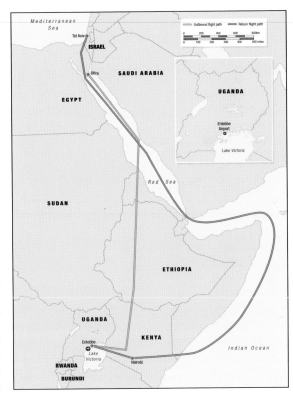

Although many had slept on the long journey home, most members of The Unit were still exhausted and emotionally drained. After unloading the Mercedes-Benz, Amitzur Kafri and Danny Dagan filled the car with other members of The Unit and returned to their base at Kfar Sirkin. There they were met by BrigGen

Karnaf 4X-FBQ 420 taxies to a halt after landing at Ben Gurion International Airport with the returning hostages.

JULY 04, 1976

0943hrs: Hostages land at Tel Nof Air Force base.

Avraham Arnan, the founder of Sayeret Matkal. He conveyed his congratulations and condolences to the soldiers. Amos Goren recalls: "When we reached the base I wasn't the slightest bit happy. Those of us at The Unit were completely removed from the whole festival that followed the operation and removed from all the publicity…What I and many others felt was hollowness." For Amir Ofer his feelings were the same: "It was the Fourth of July, the 200-year anniversary of independence in the United States. It was a very hot day and the sun was glaring in my eyes. After three nights of no sleep and extreme mental stress, after everything I had been through and all the miracles, I just wanted to be left alone. I was drained of every last drop of energy." The customary debriefing and completion of the after-action reports followed, as well as the mundane tasks of surrendering weapons and the accounting for ammunition expended. Within hours, LtCol Amiram Levine was appointed as the new commander of Sayeret Matkal. As evening drew in and the members of The Unit were finally going home, Amiram Levine passed Netanyahu's combat vest with its damaged hand grenades to Amitzur Kafri. He gave instructions for it to be destroyed. With the setting sun casting long shadows through the olive trees, Kafri

Once the rear ramp was lowered, the hostages rushed to the embrace of their waiting relatives as they were greeted with raised arms by Foreign Minister Yigal Allon. To the left of the photograph is the French airline pilot, Michel Bacos. The ecstatic welcome was a fitting climax to Operation *Thunderbolt*.

dug a small hole in the hard, packed earth and attached a small block of PE4 explosive to the vest. After retiring to a safe distance, he detonated the charge remotely. The ensuing explosion was the final act of Operation *Thunderbolt*.

After their brief stay at Tel Nof Air Base, the hostages were flown the short distance to Lod International Airport, where they received an ecstatic and emotional welcome, with the Chief Rabbi of the IDF leading the celebrations with blasts on a *shofar* (ram's horn). The hostages streamed down the rear ramp of the Hercules into the arms of their families and loved ones. Their ordeal was over. Yet for some it was never to end. Martine Maimoni recalls the moment to this day:

> For the rest of my life, I will never forget that scene in the airport. Everyone was hugging and crying. Suddenly, I heard on the loudspeaker: "The Maimoni family is requested to come to room such-and-such." We entered the room, and there they told us that Jean-Jacques had been killed during the rescue mission. My father screamed horribly. My mother fainted. Meanwhile, all around us, people were laughing.

Relatives and friends rejoice as the C-130 Karnaf carrying the hostages comes in to land at Ben Gurion International Airport near Tel Aviv. It was a moment of remarkable unity for the Israeli nation. Jonathan Rosenblum was a student in Israel at the time and recalls the tension and then the joy that filled the air on July 4: "Complete strangers were embracing on the bus. For once Jewish unity seemed like a reality, not a fundraiser's slogan. As I looked around the bus, one thought kept recurring: We are all Jews. The obvious differences between us— language, skin color, personal and familial history—suddenly seemed unimportant."

They were not alone in their loss. Aged just eight, Tzipi Cohen had witnessed her father bleeding to death before her eyes, a trauma that would remain with her for the rest of her life. To Benjamin and Iddo Netanyahu, the loss of their eldest brother would likewise haunt them all their days. His sacrifice at the moment of supreme success was a fitting end to a brilliant warrior philosopher. Two days later Yoni Netanyahu was buried with full military honors at Mount Herzl cemetery in Jerusalem. Thousands attended his funeral, and Defense Minister Peres delivered the eulogy. Until then, Yoni Netanyahu was unknown to the Israeli public because of the largely secret nature of his military assignments, but he became a national hero overnight. Schools, military camps, and scholarships were named after him. In his honor and memory, Operation *Thunderbolt* was renamed Operation *Yonatan*.

AFTERMATH

The tragedy did not end there. Soon after the raid, 75-year-old Dora Bloch was dragged from her bed in Ward 6B of Mulago Hospital by two of Amin's most notorious henchmen, Maj Farouk Minawa, the head of the dreaded State Research Bureau (SRB), and Capt Nasur Ondoga, Amin's Chief of Protocol. She was bundled screaming into the back of a black Peugeot 504 and never seen alive again. She was buried in a sugar plantation near Lugazi some 30 miles (48 km) east of Kampala. After the overthrow of Idi Amin in 1979, her remains were recovered and returned to Israel for burial.

Idi Amin's revenge knew no bounds following the humiliation inflicted by the Israeli raid on Entebbe. Even the reoccupation of the airport by the Ugandan Army had been a fiasco as Vincent Magombe, a student at the time, later recalled: "We were laughing because we saw the Ugandan Army arrive hours after the Israelis left. The troops just started shooting at anything and were even fighting each other." Indeed, it is reckoned that almost half of the 45 Ugandan soldiers killed at Entebbe were the result of fratricidal fire long after the Israelis had departed. The next victims of Amin's rage were the air traffic controllers at the airport, Lawrence Mawanda, Mohammed Muhido, and Fabian Rwengyembe. All three were dragged from the arms of their families by the SRB and taken to the Katabi army barracks at Entebbe. Mawanda was killed by having nails hammered into his head and the rest of his body was pulverized beyond recognition with sledgehammers. His colleagues suffered an equally gruesome fate. Their bodies were dumped in the Namanve Forest, one of Amin's most favored killing grounds. Because of the perceived collusion of the Kenyan government, Amin ordered the slaughter of over 3,000 Karamojong whose tribal lands straddled the disputed border between Uganda and Kenya. In a final act of vindictiveness, Idi Amin invited Bruce Mackenzie, a former security adviser to President Jomo Kenyatta and then Minister of Agriculture, on an official visit to Uganda. As a parting gift, on May 24, 1978, Amin presented him with the mounted head of an antelope. As Mackenzie's airplane passed over the Ngong Hills along the Great Rift Valley, it exploded in midair, killing all on board.

Nevertheless, Idi Amin's odious regime began to crumble after the Entebbe raid. Prior to that event, he had established a powerful army and secret police force that terrorized his people into submission, but the Entebbe crisis shattered his aura of invincibility. Nothing Amin did after that could rebuild his grip on the country. President Idi Amin was overthrown in April 1979 following the Tanzanian invasion of Uganda. He fled to Jeddah in Saudi Arabia with two wives and 24 children. Responsible for the deaths of over 300,000 people, Amin lived in quiet seclusion watching satellite television, playing the accordion, and fishing in the Red Sea. Ironically his place of exile was below the flight path used by the Israeli Air Force Karnafs that had been his nemesis. Idi Amin died on August 16, 2003, of multiple organ failure brought on by tertiary syphilis.

In the immediate aftermath of the Entebbe raid, the government of Uganda convened a session of the UN Security Council to seek international condemnation of Israel for their violation of Ugandan sovereignty. The Israeli government

The raid on Entebbe has been a rich topic for filmmakers, with the first movie appearing just months later as *Victory at Entebbe*. Directed by Marvin J. Chomsky, it starred Anthony Hopkins, Burt Lancaster, Elizabeth Taylor, and Richard Dreyfuss. In 1977, *Raid on Entebbe* was released starring Peter Finch, Horst Buchholz, Charles Bronson, Yaphet Kotto (as Idi Amin), and James Woods. The TV movie was directed by Irvin Kershner and gained nine nominations at the Emmy and Golden Globe awards. Playing Prime Minister Rabin, it was the last ever screen role of Peter Finch. It won a Golden Globe as best TV Movie of 1977. In the same year, an Israeli production *Mivtsa Yonatan* appeared with the English title of *Operation Thunderbolt*. Directed by Menahem Golan, it starred the popular singer/actor Yehoram Gaon as Yoni Netanyahu. In these three stills from the movie set, the actors are wearing the wrong uniforms and carrying the wrong weapons, but that is show business or perhaps the IDF military censor. A complete replica of the Old Terminal at Entebbe was constructed at Ben Gurion International Airport. Soon after its release,

Amitzur Kafri got married when he had just a one-night honeymoon that comprised a trip to Tel Aviv for Chinese food and to see the movie, before returning to duty. He recalls that the movie was "ridiculous," but it did remind him of the excitement and fear of Entebbe and the long hours lying by the Mercedes with his comrades on the Karnaf.

prepared for the debate as carefully as the IDF had done for the raid on Entebbe. The council chamber was packed with diplomats and journalists as Uganda's Foreign Minister, Juma Oris Abdalla, rose to initiate the debate. He launched into a lengthy diatribe against "Zionist barbarism and banditry" and followed up with a demand for full compensation for damages incurred by Uganda during the raid. As Israel's Ambassador to the UN, Chaim Herzog stood to address the chamber, which fell deathly quiet:

> I am in no way sitting in the dock as the accused party. I stand here as an accuser of this rotten, corrupt, brutal, cynical, bloodthirsty monster of international terrorism and all those who support it in one way or the other, whether by commission or omission. We come with a simple message to the Council: we are proud of what we have done because we have demonstrated to the world that, [to] a small country in Israel's circumstances, with which the members of this Council are by now all too familiar, the dignity of man, human life and human freedom constitute the highest values. We are proud not only

On the tenth anniversary of the raid, there was a reunion of the hostages and some of the military personnel that took part during Operation *Thunderbolt*. Here, Surin Hershko talks to the airline captain of Flight 139, Michel Bacos, and his wife. Hershko was paralyzed for life due to gunshot wounds and confined to a wheelchair. For his courageous decision to remain with the Jewish hostages together with his crew, Bacos was reprimanded by Air France and suspended from flying duties.

because we have saved the lives of over 100 innocent people—men, women and children—but because of the significance of our act for the cause of human freedom.

The motion was defeated.

The successful rescue of the hostages following the hijacking of Air France Flight 139 did not herald the end of this particular phenomenon of terrorism. The greatest number of casualties following an aerial hijacking occurred in the People's Republic of China on October 2, 1990. During a domestic flight from Canton to Xiamen in the Fujian Province, a Xiamen Airlines Boeing Advanced 737-247 was commandeered by a lone hijacker claiming to have explosives strapped to his body. He demanded that the aircraft be diverted to Taiwan. Due to insufficient fuel, it was necessary to land at Baiyun Airport. On the final approach an altercation broke out on the flight deck and the aircraft landed heavily, veering off the runway and hitting two further Boeings waiting for takeoff. A total of 132 people were killed and a further 50 injured. A more worrying development was the increasing use of aerial sabotage as a more effective means of terrorism. Undoubtedly the most notorious incident was the destruction of Pan American World Airways Flight 103 that exploded over Lockerbie in Scotland on December 21, 1988, killing all 259 persons on board with 11 more killed on the ground. However, the events of 9/11 (the destruction of the twin towers of the World Trade Center in New York on September 11, 2001), with the combination of aerial hijacking and sabotage through use of the plane itself, has signaled a new and more terrifying form of aerial terrorism. Indeed, it is possible to argue that the events at Entebbe and similar acts of terrorism by terrorists throughout the 1970s were a harbinger of events still to come and that all the Western powers missed an opportunity to address the root causes of this problem before it spiralled into new depths of horror in the 21st century.

Operation *Yonatan* was a defining moment in Israeli history. After the traumas of the Yom Kippur War, the Israel Defense Forces once more basked in the limelight of public approval. Thousands of workers volunteered to contribute up to a week's pay to the IDF welfare fund. A group of Haifa businessmen offered a free holiday by the sea to any of the soldiers that took part in the raid. To Sayeret Matkal, the Entebbe raid did much to expunge the perceived failures of Ma'alot and the Savoy Hotel. Everyone in Israel remembers exactly where they were when they heard of the rescue. Furthermore, it was a prime example of many disparate agencies within the military and the government working in harmony for a specific end. Israeli politics is a fractious world that often thrives on confrontation and rivalry among politicians. Failure at

Entebbe would have meant the fall of the Rabin government, but more importantly, it would have been a devastating blow to Israeli national pride and prestige.

That the operation did not fail was down to the expertise and meticulous planning of the IDF and the intelligence agencies. Almost three days were lost as a solution was sought through the international community, particularly with France as the owner of the hijacked airliner, before Israel realized that once the nationals of other countries had been freed, it stood alone. By that Thursday, the Israeli people were resigned to the prospect of surrender in exchange for the hostages' lives. Yet concerted and coordinated planning for a military solution then ensued, with the Israeli Air Force providing the impetus and the means for the mission, while Sayeret Matkal refined the hostage rescue plan. In this, they were ably supported by Sayeret Tzanhanim and Sayeret Golani as Mossad teams prepared the ground in East Africa. That such a complex plan could be developed in such a short time over so great a distance is remarkable. The execution of the operation was almost flawless. At all levels of command, from the prime minister to the humblest medical orderly, and from the chief of staff to the soldier of The Unit with a Kalashnikov standing face to face with a terrorist, each performed to the best of their ability and prevailed despite the tragic losses. Moreover, the fundamental reason for the success was surprise, both strategically and tactically. At the strategic level, no one, least of all the PFLP–SOG planners, believed that the reach of the IDF could extend so far (which was why Uganda had been chosen as the destination for the hostages in collusion with Idi Amin). At the tactical level, the use of an "official" Mercedes-Benz with escorts as a subterfuge was inspired. It allowed The Unit to close with the enemy and eliminate the terrorists in a matter of seconds. In the words of former Prime Minister Ariel Sharon:

> There are few military operations which, in retrospect, reflect the spirit and courage of an entire nation. Operation *Yonatan* was one of those few. There are few commanders who, during their lifetime and even more so after their death, become a symbol of a heroic and confident Israel, a peace-seeking nation, determined to confront its enemies, through dedication and adherence to the cause. This is how the late Col Yonatan Netanyahu—Yoni—who fell during the battle to release the Entebbe hostages, is engraved in our national memory. Operation *Yonatan* is perhaps also a reminder of a time when we were younger and smaller, but had the courage, imagination and determination to spread our wings…

The raid on Entebbe stands as one of the great achievements of the IDF, almost biblical in its scale and success in saving the hostages. Sarah Davidson wrote after the ordeal: "There is a verse, 'The Lord's redemption comes like the twinkling of an eye.' When we heard the sudden shooting I repeated the Shema Yisrael, which a Jew says when their hour has come. And a soldier leapt toward me with Hebrew on his tongue. I felt goose pimples. I would not die, but live to tell the deeds of the Lord!"

The raid on Entebbe was successfully completed on July 4, 1976, the bicentennial of Independence Day in the United States of America; a country based on the principle of liberty and freedom for all men and women. The passengers of Flight 139 who returned to Israel in a C-130 Hercules experienced the true meaning of the word freedom on that day. The raid on Entebbe must rank as one of the greatest Special Forces missions ever. It proved what could be achieved by a democracy in the face of international terrorism. As so eloquently expressed by Iddo Netanyahu, the brother of Yoni: "The raid on Entebbe touched the souls of men and women across the globe in the most fundamental way possible. For it proved that at least once, even against inconceivable odds, justice could be done and right could win."

GLOSSARY

armada A fleet of ships, usually in military formation as they prepare to go into battle.

assassination The targeted killing of a public figure, usually for political purposes.

barbarism A display of acts, attitudes, or ideas that are primitive, crude, or inappropriate.

bicentennial A 200th anniversary or its celebration.

casualty A victim, usually in a military situation, who is killed or injured.

communiqué An official report or statement, usually issued by a public agency.

confiscate To seize by authority.

cordially With deep sincerity.

dictator A ruler who assumes absolute power and authority.

fedayeen Distinct militant groups and individuals who identify themselves as freedom fighters, particularly in the Middle East.

gentile A non-Jewish person.

grenade A weapon that is thrown or launched at an enemy and explodes a short time after release.

hijacking The unlawful seizure of an aircraft by an individual or group.

hostage A person who is held by a captor, usually until the captor's demands are met.

jihad A religious duty of Muslims, a personal struggle in devotion to Islam; can also be interpreted as a holy war waged on behalf of Islam.

maneuver A military strategy or movement designed to give one side an advantage.

paratroopers Soldiers trained to parachute from an airplane.

publicity Media attention to a person or event, sometimes used as a marketing tool.

reconnaissance A scouting mission used to collect information.

squadron A small unit or formation of military persons, aircraft, or warships.

terrorism The systematic use of terror as means of coercion; sometimes violent acts are perpetrated to create fear in the public.

FOR MORE INFORMATION

Israel Defense Forces History Museum
Tel Aviv Promenade
Kaufman Street and Hamered Street
Tel Aviv, Israel
Web site: http://ilmuseums.com
A collection of films, maps, historical documents, and other exhibits dedicated to preserving the history of the Israeli Army.

The Jewish Museum
1109 5th Avenue
New York, NY 10128
(212) 423-3200
Web site: http://www.thejewishmuseum.org
A museum dedicated to preserving 4,000 years of art and Jewish culture.

Ministry of Foreign Affairs
9 Yitzhak Rabin Boulevard
Kiryat Ben-Gurion
Jerusalem 91035
Web site: http://www.mfa.gov.il
Government ministry of Israel dedicated to diplomacy and foreign affairs.

Museum of Jewish Heritage
Edmond J. Safra Plaze
36 Battery Place
New York, NY 10280
Web site: http://www.mjhnyc.org
(646) 437-4200
Museum dedicated to Jewish heritage and the holocaust.

The Uganda Museum
5-7 Kira Road
POB 365 Kampala
Uganda
Web site: http://www.ugandatourism.org
A collection of cultural and historical exhibitions representing Uganda.

Web Sites

Due to the changing nature of Internet links, Rosen Publishing has developed an online list of Web sites related to the subject of this book. This site is updated regularly. Please use this link to access the list:

http://www.rosenlinks.com/raid/isra

FOR FURTHER READING

Chasnoff, Joel. *The 188th Crybaby Brigade: A Skinny Jewish Kid from Chicago Fights Hezbollah: A Memoir.* New York, NY: Simon & Schuster, 2010.

Drory, Ze'ev. *The Israel Defence Force and the Foundation of Israel.* New York, NY: Routledge, 2005.

Gerald, Eddie (photographer). *Jerusalem and the Holy Land.* New York, NY: DK, 2007.

Gordis, Daniel. *Saving Israel: How the Jewish People Can Win a War That May Never End.* Hoboken, NJ: Wiley, 2009.

Harms, Gregory, and Todd M. Ferry. *The Palestine-Israel Conflict: A Basic Introduction.* 2nd ed. London, England: Pluto, 2008.

Mearsheimer, John J., and Stephen M. Walt. *The Israel Lobby and U.S. Foreign Policy.* New York, NY: FSG, 2008.

Netanyahu, Iddo, *Entebbe: A Defining Moment in the War on Terrorism—The Jonathan Netanyahu Story.* Noble, OK: Balfour, 2003.

Netanyahu, Iddo and Yoram Hazony (trans). *Yoni's Last Battle: The Rescue at Entebbe 1976.* Jerusalem, Israel: Gefen Publishing, 2001.

Netanyahu, Jonathan. *The Letters of Jonathan Netanyahu: The Commander of the Entebbe Rescue Force.* Jerusalem, Israel: Gefen Publishing, 2001.

Rubinger, David. *Israel Through My Lens: Sixty Years as a Photojournalist.* New York, NY: Abbeville Press, 2008.

Sachar, Howard M. *A History of Israel: From the Rise of Zionism to Our Time.* New York, NY: Knopf, 2007.

Sofer, Barbara. *Keeping Israel Safe: Serving in the Israel Defense Forces.* Minneapolis, MN: Lerner, 2008.

BIBLIOGRAPHY

Betser, Col. Muki, with Robert Rosenberg. *Secret Soldier.* New York, NY: Simon & Schuster, 1996.

Gazit, Major General Shlomo. Monograph. *International Security*, Vol. 6, No. 1 (Summer 1981), President and Fellows of Harvard College and the Massachusetts Institute of Technology.

Gero, David. *Flights of Terror: Aerial Hijack and Sabotage Since 1930.* Somerset, England: Patrick Stephens, Ltd., 1997.

Harclerode, Peter. *Secret Soldiers: Special Forces in the War Against Terrorism.* London, England: Cassell & Co, 2000.

McRaven, William H. *Spec Ops: Case Studies in Special Operations Warfare: Theory and Practice.* New York, NY: Presidio, 1995.

Netanyahu, Iddo. *Entebbe: The Jonathan Netanyahu Story.* Noble, OK: Balfour Books, 2003.

Netanyahu, Iddo. *Yoni's Last Battle: The Rescue at Entebbe, 1976.* Jerusalem, Israel: Gefen Publishing, 2002.

Williams, Maj. (Res.) Louis. "Entebbe Diary." *IDF Journal*, Vol. II, No. 3.

INDEX

ABOUT THE AUTHOR

Simon Dunstan is a well-established author, film-maker, and photographer in the field of military history. He specializes in armored warfare, and has written on this subject for two decades. His books have covered topics such as helicopter and armored warfare in Vietnam, the Challenger main battle tank, the British Guards, and armored warfare in Korea. Simon lives and works in London.